FATHER JOHN SAMMON

CHRIST UNCONQUERED

UNCON

CHRIST QUERED

By ARTHUR LITTLE, S. J.

ILLUSTRATED BY FRITZ KREDEL

INTRODUCTION BY FULTON OURSLER

PRENTICE-HALL, INC., NEW YORK

De licentia Superiorum Ordinis:

IOANNES R. MACMAHON, S.J.,
Praep. Prov. Hib. Soc. Jesu.

Die 14° Decembris, 1944.

Nihil Obstat:

IOANNES KELLY,
Censor. Theol. Deput.

Imprimi potest:

✠ IOANNES CAROLUS,
Archiep. Dublinen.,
Hiberniae Primas.

Dublini, die 19° Martii, 1945.

FIRST AMERICAN EDITION

PRINTED IN THE UNITED STATES OF AMERICA

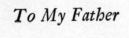

To My Father

The supreme sacredness of my theme has constrained me to conform to historical truth in substance and especially to avoid wilful distortion of Our Lord's purpose in the Passion. But in the poem some few historical details have been changed and fictitious episodes added for the purposes of construction or of stressing certain significances. Moreover, certain speculative conclusions have been stated with an air of certainty, though they are indeed no more than conjectures and may on scrutiny be found false. It concerns me here to take precautions lest my readers attribute to me, as considered convictions, what are but the instantaneous suggestions received while the imagination was rehearsing the stages of an action. This work is a poem, not an historical monograph; it aims directly only at poetic truth, not at formal truth of which historical truth is a species.

It only remains for me here to express my gratitude to, amongst others, Fr. J. Bolland, S.J., and to Fr. C. Mulcahy, S.J., who saw the opening lines. Without their encouragement the work might never have been completed, without their advice it would not have been even as good as it is.

TULLABEG.

ix

CONTENTS

xi

INTRODUCTION

WHEN Aristotle, greatest of Greek critics, spoke of the purification of the human spirit through tragedy, he wrote beyond his time and better than he knew. In his day, the consummate tragedy and the complete purification were yet to come. The story of Our Lord's Crucifixion, the divine tragedy that is the sequel to the mortal tragedy of Adam, finds us all suppliant at the foot of the Cross. Confronted with this mighty theme, artists and poets are inspired to their best. What subject could be greater? With what hero would we more gladly identify ourselves, even in His extreme agony, than Jesus Christ? Life itself becomes a preparation for that mystery. The deepest love possible to men is their willingness to share in the divine tragedy, even without forethought of the Resurrection that shall raise them up to where all tragedy must have an end.

Christ Unconquered, the title of the present poem on this vast subject, implies the triumph of the Resurrection but closes with the descent from the Cross. In any work of art or literature such a theme demands reverence, eloquence, and almost angelic good taste. These qualities are apparent in Father Little's epic on the Crucifixion and the events leading up to it. In addition, the story moves with the excitement necessary for effective narration. Familiar as the material is, we yield to the suspense in a kind of hopeless hope that the dread climax may be averted, that the Master may, after all, shine forth in His imperishable glory and put His dark foes to rout.

The poem will prove deeply moving to all who know and acknowledge the central facts of Christianity. The dialogue, touchstone of a work dealing with holy things, is expertly handled. It reveals shrewd insight into the lesser characters, and the speeches assigned to Our Lord are reverently simple and within the definition of His divine intent:

> *To your authority*
> *Honor, and to your question I am king*
> *Though not of this world. See, the kings of earth*
> *Have those who will defend them: I have none,*
> *But come to men as one by nature framed*
> *For sacrifice, to take their absolute will*
> *As it were God's. I am the first of things,*
> *Intelligence; my everlasting realm*
> *Far from the visitations of the sun*
> *And the fixed change that is time's governor*
> *Resides. There neither any night nor noon*
> *Has sway, but knowledge full that lulls desire*
> *To quiet at its home is to each mind*
> *Its own intrinsic day unwavering,*
> *And calls up in the being of the mind*
> *Its own sufficient world; all spirits there*

Live wakeful with excess of their own light
Which is the view of God. My heritage
Sets me with the eternal; neither death,
Nor change, nor time, nor matter can fulfil
Subjects of incorruptible sovereignty.

This passage from the dialogue between Jesus and Pilate illustrates Father Little's method of expanding, without altering, the substance of Our Lord's words.

The poem is divided into ten books, and in treatment and style inescapably recalls Milton's *Paradise Lost*. Books I, II, and IX open with formal invocations in the classic manner. In Book I, against the background of ancient Palestine, murmurous with the past and with forebodings of the future, the Sanhedrin are gathered in the High Priest's house to discuss ways and means for the destruction of Jesus Christ. The midnight scene, echoing and horrible, except for the gentler voice of Gamaliel, reminds one of the convening of the fallen angels in Milton's maserpiece. Annas, the High Priest, embodiment of pride and false logic is quite clearly the counterpart of Satan. With Annas' command: "Judas, we wait your voice!" the divine tragedy is set in motion, and the reader feels once more the tightening of nerves and heart that never fails to accompany the first announcement of the theme of fatality. Thereafter, the story moves inexorably onward, following the known pattern, but with much valid imaginative detail.

The technique is also suggestive of Milton. The blank verse is Miltonic throughout, built up in large paragraphs to a sounding climax. As with Milton, sentences start within a line more often than at the beginning, and the syntax overflows from line to line in a cascade of enjambment wherein the single metrical units are like smaller ripples on one huge, advancing wave. Miltonic, too, are the frequent place-names used to enrich the verse by sonority and association, the high rhetorical diction where elevation of tone is essential, and the numerous classical allusions. Such devices are most appropriate in setting the background; near the beginning of the poem the flavor of old Palestine is conveyed thus:

> *Eastward from Ascalon,*
> *Once pledged to serve the Fish-god and his rites,*
> *And Ashdod where the enchanted Philistines*
> *Had vowed under the moon of Astaroth*
> *And slain their babes, and from the Tyrian shore*
> *Others set out in slow and devious files,*
> *Where the Phoenician traders gathered bales*
> *Of woven purple and bestrode the foam*
> *In laden galleys bound for Sicily*
> *And the Ionian Sea. Many had sought*
> *The confines of their fathers from afar,*
> *From Edom and from Moab and from lone*
> *Palmyra and disastrous Babylon,*
> *Ecbatana and Ninus, cities haught,*
> *And from the flood where Alexandria*
> *Ruled the divided waters, and from Rome*
> *Invincible, the mistress of the world*
> *And thief of Israel.*

The classic spirit finds echoes in this poem as well as the classic allusion, perhaps most markedly the spirit of Virgil and of Latin verse, that so swayed Milton's muse and Dante's before him. In general structure this influence contributes to compression of material within a limited space and period

of time: Jerusalem and Holy Week. Evenness of tempo
and the observance of due proportion are also classical at-
tributes. The elaborate Virgilian simile is not frequently
encountered, however; as a rule, Father Little prefers the
brief metaphor:

> *Dreamer upon the solitary isle*
> *That harvests the marched fields of ocean's pearls.*

Occasionally we find a more elaborate figure:

> *Here on the patient tables of my mind*
> *Scored by the style that works their vacancy*
> *With figured knowledge, or by subtler touch*
> *Or natural instruction of the sense*
> *Induced, in other places and new hands*
> *The tale divine unfolds.*

With this organ of many stops before him, Father Little
sounds the music of his poem, and amid its harmonies we
can forget the instrument, interesting though it is. We pass
from artistry to art that involves us in the steps to Calvary,
the Last Words, and the descent from the Cross. When
the tragedy has reached its conclusion, Mary, the Blessed
Mother, lingers with us even as she lingered by the Cross
on that first Good Friday. At the beginning of Book IX
the poet invokes her as Queen of Heaven:

> *Mother of God, mother of man reborn,*
> *Majestic woman, who at the bitter tree*
> *Besought the burden of the motherhood*
> *Of men by immolation of your heart*
> *To bear his pangs whom you had given to them,*
> *And, by his gift of men, spoils of his pain,*

> *To you, received your children to consort*
> *With him, your only son, as you consort,*
> *Remember that award!*

This touching bit of description will more deeply move the heart of the average reader:

> *Mary the Virgin, straight and slender-knit,*
> *Sat with her hands upon her lap composed;*
> *On her cold cheek lay winter unreproved,*
> *And from her eyes still feeling, conscious pain*
> *At ease within the hospitable haven*
> *Of the accomplice heart, looked quiet out*
> *Nor wrung one shudder from the graven lips;*
> *But sorrow greeted had infused a calm*
> *More royal than the fabulous repose*
> *Distilled from changeless mirth in those bright dreams*
> *That were the golden gods; so waited she,*
> *Passive and unappalled, on twilight grey*
> *And the fell mystery of approaching time.*

Toward the end of the poem, the Blessed Mother speaks for us all:

> *Let us shorten mourning now*
> *Since the whole heaven is in festival*
> *This day at the high prowess of the cross*
> *And let us to our offices to bind*
> *His limbs with homage for his lonely rest,*
> *For he was royal and dies but for a space.*

Having copied these words, I put down Father Little's poem with a sense of gratitude to a writer who has had the courage to choose the most important theme in the universe for his epic and the patient skill to present it once again for contemplation. The winter evening is falling, the trees in the Park are black against the red sky, and all the huge city is lighted for Christmastide. For some hours now, I have been far away from winter and Christmas; I have been in the Palestine of nearly twenty centuries ago, my mind at one with Lent and Holy Week. But, as I emerge again into present reality, to the confusion of a modern city in my ears, and the confusion of a ruinous world on the fringe of my thoughts, I understand how Holy Week and Christmas are essentially one and the same. Beyond the Christmas lights I see the shadow of the Cross, and beyond the Cross, the unutterable glory of the Resurrection. From any fine work dedicated to the Passion of Our Lord we proceed to the thought of our own dedication to His everlasting rebirth in the forgiveness of our sins and in the stillness of our hearts. *Adeste, fideles!*

FULTON OURSLER

CHRIST UNCONQUERED

Smite me, O God, with your earth-darkening light!
Intelligence, undo this night of sense
That blinds my spirit to the spiritual
And give my wit your truth! For now I sing
Your stoop heroic from your lonely seat
And everlasting into manly flesh,
Man to redeem, with agony for arms
And death your victory. Break through my lips,
Eternal Mind, quicken this flight of verse
With fiery breath divine, that your dear strife
May by its incantation live again
In image and yourself within men's hearts!
Yours be the burden now, though mine the voice.

Three years after the thirty hidden deep
In peaceful Nazareth had Christ the Lord
Walked openly the fields of Palestine,
When that remorseless band that brewed his fall
Assembled by command of the High Priest

3

Within his house, there to debate what sleight
Might bare the scope of hate. These were the days
When the thrice-broken might of Israel
Remembered its lost greatness and in grief
Took hope of mighty God's old federacy,
Of Pharaoh drowned and all his mailed men,
Of the waste strewn with manna, and the walls
Of Jericho felled with a clarion-peal.
To Salem ravished came the stricken race
Innumerable from many lands and far
Once tributary or oppressive now,
Pensive they came and wroth, to slay their herds,
And eat the bitter herbs memorial,
And brood on wars redemptive. Troops had come
From the Ten Cities and from Galilee's
Soft-foliaged slopes and dim and odorous streams
And many a town of fat-tilthed Galaad,
Ramoth, and Pella, and Mahanaim,
And from invidious Ephraim, the thorn
That lamed the foot of Juda when in its need
The usurping king forswore obedience
And lit the emulous and undying fire
On Bethel's altar. Eastward from Ascalon,
Once pledged to serve the Fish-god and his rites,
And Ashdod where the enchanted Philistines
Had vowed under the moon of Astaroth
And slain their babes, and from the Tyrian shore
Others set out in slow and devious files,
Where the Phoenician traders gathered bales
Of woven purple and bestrode the foam
In laden galleys bound for Sicily

5

And the Ionian Sea. Many had sought
The confines of their fathers from afar,
From Edom and from Moab and from lone
Palmyra and disastrous Babylon,
Ecbatana and Ninus, cities haught,
And from the flood where Alexandria
Ruled the divided waters, and from Rome
Invincible, the mistress of the world
And thief of Israel. So all these wound
Like shadows through the labyrinthine streets
Of the sad mother-city, rapt and grave
With meditative steps more populous
And murmurous than are the Syrian bees
That swarm upon a bough in Carmel, fast
About their chosen queen, and all the fronds
Are shaken with the passion of their zeal
And loud with savage dronings.

                                    But that day
The presage of untimely sacrifice
And stir of deeds untoward had moved the crowds
With new unrest, as from the Temple steps
They heard the herald of the priests proclaim
Christ outlawed and the right to slay conferred
On each who should behold. They heard and passed
On with bent brows, weighing the Godlike deeds
Of succor strong that some had seen, all knew;
But as men use, prone to believe the worst
Of men, lest they themselves be found too light
In the same scales, they eyed the sterner view
And kept the poise of judgment.

6

The downy glow of evening, husbanding
Its bosomed flush, sank from the halted clouds
And laced the cedar groves with wandering warmth,
The herding bondsman lone on the wild downs
Tolled to his sluggish flock and homeward led
Slant by the brows of shadow-freaked fells
Into the wattled fold. And in the brake
Of bramble creeping and the tangled vine
The last slow chuckle of the drowsy birds
Made hollower the next silence. Presently
Before the feet of night the desert woods
That stared the walls afar, lay in repose,
Abandoned bowers; beyond the pilgrim cells
All was as still as when Saint Ezra rose
By steps laborious out of haunted glooms
Of forests perilous and envious tribes
And viewed the waste of the Babylonian rape,
Fair edifices, to corruption hurled
By flight of those that quickened them, possessed
By silence and immobile images,
Save when the visiting wind with uncouth breath
Sighed like the tidings of the funeral plaint
Of Magians for King Darius dead
In Iran by the streams of Ispahan.

But in the High Priest's house a heavy hush
Far other than the pause that beckons sleep
Hung pregnant, a taut silence as of war
In leash and deeds that waited but the call
Of apt occasion. There the Sanhedrin

Sat tense with purpose, close about their chief,
With eyes illegible as if each soul
Lived but to guard its secret; only showed
Their corded brows and grave, deliberate gests
The impending act. Them in full session met,
Awaiting counsel, Caiaphas addressed:
"I have no counsel for you, Israel,
To stem your terrors, none but his advice
Who guides when beggared are our other minds,
And prompts this conclave, menaced and contemned
By an inferior foe, now to erase
Its peril. Annas, advise!"
     And Annas stood
Confronting them as he confronted once
His heart's indictments, unappalled, until
Disuse had stilled it. And with choler reined
He these to them: "Not now, Synod august,
O Peers of Israel, not now the time
To shun the deed long purposed and approved,
Now, when the hour desired invites to strike,
To hold the hand, feigning for justice' sake
To shrink from what we fear, whose cause was vouched
With the archaic bases of the world.
God who of old founded the firmament
Founded therewith as firmly on our sires
This Church and Law; and we, his chosen priests,
Are his vice-gerents; who opposes us,
Opposes God. Therefore this serf who dares
To pluck the prop of our authority,
The people's worship, and by pattern teach
The hardihood to judge us, is by God

Committed to our vengeance; if we fail,
God fails and we fail God. Abandon prayer
And give your thoughts to deeds! For oft we find
That after prayer we fail, or all achieved
Then is the issue seen to be the fruit
Of fortune or our single selves; nay, men
Whose blasphemies have quenched the fiery faith
Of martyrs in the mold have conquered crowns
And added realm to realm. Only the mind
That fears no truth, the will that makes its end,
The hand to the will faithful, are on earth
Infallible allies; let these be ours
And let who will chide our victorious deed
When we clasp fit occasion. And this night
Breeds the occasion and must bear our deed
When comes the Nazarene within the walls
To eat the Pasch, lest absence start surmise
Of infidelity to God whose law
He apes to practice. Never must he quit
These city walls. How to detect, how hold,
How swing the multitude and Rome to will
With us his due extinction undelayed,
Immune from heritage of enmity,
All is determined, am I seconded
By your unswerving valor. If we seize
Men will as ever scorn the captive one,
Hate him for trust once given, squandered now,
And hold the victor just, for they place right
Where they divine their thrift. Light then our task
To sway the vengeful folk so to exact
His killing that the deed may seem their act,

Our act their motion; nor can Rome evade
The general will. So to lay hold is first
And all the conduct of the issue lies
Within our power. Now ours to choke remorse
The pampered bantling of infirm design
And pity, its ally, whose shrill complaint
Thwarts resolution and the craven hides
Under the guise of nature; Christ retains
No private rights against the institutes
Of public safety by the act of God
Decreed immutably. Be our intent
Sole law to each, and I sole reckoner;
I, by unrighteous conqueror overthrown
Unrighteously, when impious Gratus schemed
To hurl me from my seat, unvanquished still
I am your god in law, and godlike now
I here prescribe the right, trusting alone
In my unyielding hand to lead our strife
To my fixed end. I stand before you here
Constant of my just cause, franchised in heart
To plead it soon with bloody argument;
Only the pledges of who scorn to be
Pale renegades unto our heavenly charge
Fail me for execution. Now, your oaths!"

He paused; but they all blenched regarded him,
Fearing him so that they feared more to flee;
Only Gamaliel, the sage, arose
Swiftly in anger at the extorting guile
And said to them: "O dupes of your desires,
Not love of truth but hatred of all truth

Save what you see, and will to prove most just
What most you will, have made impassioned plea
Against God in your hearts. The Nazarene,
Though young and suddenly, by prowess rare
And semblance of an inborn majesty
Has won allegiance such as we have won
Hardly by industry and sedulous years;
Thence is this irk, that we, though loth to see,
Must see perforce, betrayed by counterpoise,
Our worth inferior, and to him begrudge
Being, who by his being shortens ours.
And, since we lightly by desire suborned
Esteem the power we owe to base its right
On God's investiture, we represent
In challenge to our state contempt of God's
Feigned ordinance, in envious murdering
Defense of God's prescription. Envy thus
Lives not in us but with deceit of self
And reason bribed to advocate our cause,
Till, fashioning an idol of the Lord
Of our ambition, we to serve him think
Whenso we serve ourselves. But nought avails
The vindication of our right contrived
By venal reason; truth stands fast, unchanged
By the reluctant will or disbelief
Or all the engines of our violence,
The only absolute impregnably;
But we who disbelieve are changed and marred
And signed for ruin. Wherefore we are just
If Christ be spurious, and our cause is God's;
But be he the divine deliverer

Of Sion, the Messiah from of old
Prophesied to our fathers, then our hands
War with almighty foes. Better to waive
Purpose unjust and perish than to attain
Dominion with unrighteous arms. Our task
Is first not to condemn but to discern
If Jesus be the Saviour; but you fear
To question lest the truth discerned should show
Deserved his censures and your primacy
Supplanted by the Lord. Idolaters
Of self, it is not well to fear the truth,
Nor better with delight to live a lie
Than know the truth with sadness; the worst doom
Is that which strikes and leaves the sense unchanged,
Unwitting. But if you disdain your guilt
Disdain not too the havoc that ensues,
Soon to be felt. If Jesus be the Christ
Then is he aided by the constant God,
Nor we nor all the tyrannies of earth
Can stay his purpose or delay his steps
With all our iron chains; and the attempt
On innocence unknown to be corrupt
Devotes us to the inexorable fate
Determined to the fugitives from truth
By law immutable, and our high sway
To dissolution in the destined hour
Of the inevitable chastisement,
Inevitable, though delayed."
                                        So he,
And tarried frowning, but a murmur deep
Not of applause but of resentment rose

Command me now or kill me!"
                                    Judas paused,
But cold replied the pontiff scorning him:
"Lightly I brook the hate that turns to act
Of my own purpose; wherefore, Judas, take
These thirty silver pieces, recompense
Worthy of you and him you sell. To-night
You shall instruct our arms to find the pass
To his retreat that we may thence unden
Him and his troop. Inform us now and guide!"
Then answered Judas: "Be it so! Revenge
Ekes out reward, and that you now command
What most I crave lightens obedience.
This hour in yonder house he with us twelve
Sat supping, and but now they have gone forth
Without the walls to seek the bleak ravine
Of Kedron, there to watch, a place most apt
For your arrest; men tell of its alarums,
How the dank gloom hangs on the ravenous eyes
Of the dead envious of our life, the air
Trembles with alien whisper and the dread
Rumor of unimaginable wings;
There may you act unheeded. Give me men,
A score in arms, and ere the midnight fall
I shall confront him, single him with kiss,
And leave him to your hand to work your will
Upon his guilt." And as he silent stood
Annas said softly to the sage and smiled:
"Gamaliel, you are answered."
                                    But forthwith
One started up and cried: "Annas, forbear!

Undo this bond, nor of this proselyte
Of perfidy and malice to his kind
Be fellow in iniquity! Ill fits
And ill it bodes that we on whom has flowed
Sometime the unction of the Lord should truck
With traitors." And again another cried:
"Let us take counsel first if there indeed
Be nought divine in him or sanctified,
Lest we shed blood vindictive!" And at once
With sudden panic smitten all they rose
Among themselves contending, or apart
Muttering distrust, or, the majority,
Anguished with care and terror-born surmise
Of the particular peril pending now
The private state of each, with query wroth
Besetting him straight to illuminate
The doubtful issue of their deed, who sole
Was master of his mind; and uproar swelled
And bellowed hollow in the lofty vaults,
Of policies, misgivings, or applause,
Or of unreasoned rage. Sudden arose
Annas from moment's thought and, with great voice
Outcrying clear the turmoil, peremptorily
Ordered their silence. And upon the word
Hands dropped, and voices died, and eyes stayed held
In expectation fierce, while he began
With strength and specious wit to shape their minds,
Plastic from doubt:
                         "O grave and judging House,
Lords of the passionless high Sanhedrin,
Have you forgot the noble port of calm

All undismayed and purpose undeterred,
Whereby you would confront with equal mien
Things adverse or felicitous? Long since
We have weighed all, devised our course to crush
Imposture on our rule. But comes a point
In every fell emprise when every path
Seems set with traverse and precarious;
Then the heroic heirs of destiny
Choose of all ways the surest, and attack
With heart as uncompunctious and secure
As if the prize were promised; they who quail
While yet they are in motion to achieve
Defeat their lightest aim. Now in the act
Of seizing shall we pause? Here stands our tool;
Nought needs but to apply; but if we shrink
One moment then the Nazarene prevails
And our prestige, the substance of our might,
Totters to ruin and we are dethroned.
It is most visible that this fatal night
Is pregnant with our fall or with our rise
To new access of glory. On our act
The future waits; now that the foe lies set
For apprehension, strike we or endure
The fall that follows mercy. Can you brook
The triumph of this carpenter who dares
To stir the fetid rabble round the ears
Of us, the heirs of kings, in whom the blood
Of the divinest dynasty on earth
Courses superbly? O, concede it not
Nor tramp in dust your glory's seed! I swear
By all the iron heroes of old fame

Whose greatness battened on their ruthless breasts,
By David's scythe-toothed chariots, and the nail
That Jaël buried in the oppressive brow,
By Josue who sacked tremendous Hai
And on the bloody trunks of twenty kings
Builded our laureled nation, by the sword
Of Judith, and the passion of redress
That stung Jehu to tear false Jezabel,
By Samson's pauseless arm and the eagle swoop
Of Machabaeus, by all that enmity
Unpitying whose wane has loosed our sway
And bowed our ancient pride, this night to slake
The lust for earthly immortality,
Which is the only sure, to fashion straight
A mighty story for the wondering
Of ages yet unborn, to put our names
Flush with renown for men of curveless will.
Sheer from this moment, all discussion past,
We bend to steadfast act, and in the pen
Of every motion on the execution
Grow unreflecting instruments of law,
Cold as the grey Eumenides that hound
Uneager and inflexible all days
The vestiges of guilt, until the hour
Predestined bears them to the fugitive
And they must do the doom. Endue you now
With deadly purpose, for with one accord
This moment we unleash our powers in hand.
Summon the captain of the Guard!"
                                        He ceased;
But they with a great shout vowed their accord,

Moved to one mind by the one dread, provoked
And rendered urgent by the spell of speech,
That all their high estate was jeopardous,
Only to be redeemed by instant stroke,
Daring and pitiless; forgetting all,
They brooded this alone with dazzled minds
And fed with hate their purpose. All were taut,
Tranquil in full resolve, when presently
Entered the captain of the Temple Guard
Their conference. Annas gave sharp command:
"Take all your men-at-arms and what resource
You have late levied, and with warrant firm
Seek out ere dawn Jesus, the Nazarene,
And him detain in bonds. Here is your guide
Who knows the rebel's hiding; follow him,
And whom he shall confront, single with kiss,
And leave unto your hand, him apprehend
And carry captive. Straight dispatch the task,
For on it hangs your office!" Annas then
Drew near and spoke in secret: "Once in hand,
Lead him forthwith into my dwelling-house
For a first interrogative!" The man
Bowed low and straight was gone.
                                          But in the close
He slipped the tether from his steed and leaped
Clear to the saddle, and against his rear
Fast mounted the betrayer. At a prick
The great horse pawed the sounding flints and sped
With rhythmic ring of hoofs reverberant
Snorting upon the street. The twilit trains
Of homing pilgrims gave and after gazed,

Surmising on the prelude to dire acts.
But riding they divined the consequence,
Aware, though loth to know, of their intent,
By violence extorted from the will
Against itself reluctant, by their deed
To thwart the sovereign providence of things,
Law, by whose hand all happiness endures;
And gradual fear begot dread images
Of nameless angers gathered in pursuit,
The vengeance of the universal world
By their revolt thrust from the reign of good,
Cold, deadly, pitiless, ineluctable.
So the grim riders drove with reckless rein
And flight so level that the vying winds
Seemed breathless, while upon their spirits' ears
Beat elemental chase; coursers more swift
Than Pegasus or the twin flaming yoke
That once Elias bore now seemed to strain
Neck and neck at their side, to foil their aim
Contending it with soul invincible
And indefatigable thews. Before
With perils of illusion was beset,
With thunderbolt, and earthquake, and eclipse,
The meed of who should harm the Son of God,
But the insistence of divine pursuit
Vengeful upon their heels made these seem light
In counterpoise. So in their fluttering cloaks
Panted the wind, and from the charger's shoes
Sparks crackled in the dusk, and the fell chase
Fantastic, but made real to belief
By the creative horror of their deed,

Globed their disastrous eyes. Sudden they struck
Slant on the flank of Acra, and at length
The captain from the halted beast down sprang
And, to the guard-room striding, on the horn
There winded the assembly with one blast
Not loud but long, and to the waiting ears
Charged with force peremptory. No such call
Nor to such fearful venture had evoked
Or voice or trumpet in the round of time
Since Lucifer on the embattled peak
Had hurled defiant fanfare from his host
Upon the throne of God, and troubled birth
Brought to the world's rebellion.

                                    At the call
There issued from the dark of the great fane
An uncouth armament, some few with lance
And casque and corselet geared; but many more,
New musters banded by impress from waifs
Or thieves by sale of service for their lives,
All desperate, so fearless, swelled the host
With forms unkempt and monstrous. Many realms
And many generations tallied there;
Men in their strength and boys and elders borne
From Edom and Perea and from Ur
And desolate Araby, and many a land
Known only to its own, in garbs diverse
In hue and line as were the waterweeds
That the witched fisher on the Alban Lake
Saw the lean nymphs bind on their ruddy locks,
Now stood in ranks confused and murmured fierce
In multitudinous tongues. And from the caves

And nearer hovels dimly stole in haste
A rout, eager on cruel spectacle
To slake the hunger of the fantasy,
Until the lank limbs of the holy mount
Teemed with the clusters of the populace
That dropped to the dusk outskirts of the guard
In turmoil shadowy. Restless were all
And covetous; such hosts are said to throng
On the wan banks of Lethe when the scent
Of living breath sharpens the pined desire
Of the chill dead for one more warm caress
From a love-kindled hand and the sweet air
Of this delightful earth; yet no embrace
Brings to their flowless veins the kindly heat,
Nor boots their wailing but to bare the walls
Eternal of insuperable death.

Then spoke the captain: "Men of Israel,
We go to snare the foe of Israel,
Jesus of Nazareth; now forward soft!"
Upon the word the throng were seized with fear
Inexplicable and amazement strong
That held them moveless, but, when turned the guard,
Enthralled with glamor of the chase the rest
Forgot their fear and followed. Now the night
Sent forth her starry outriders and glow
Of moonrise shook the shadows in the east
And flung cold sheets of pearl upon the sleep
Of men at peace in weariness. But lay
No rest on the disheveled company
That hung round Judas (by new terror urged

To push the fixed intent to the dark last),
And trod the narrow ways with ceaseless hum
Of bated voices and of shuffled steps
And torches tossing their resounding manes,
All truckling to the zest to see at bay
One helpless to retort. Eddied the mob
Like flotsam on a flooded stream, the forms
Of soldiery deploy forsaken clean,
Until they broached a gate and poured upon
The Vale of Hinnom, where beyond control
They thridded fast the boulders that lay piled
In disarray forbidding, and made face
Upon the road to Olivet.

                        Meanwhile
The councilors within the High Priest's house
Kept vigil tense, and each with each communed,
Distraught in waiting knots. But Caiaphas
With Annas in the trees beneath the night
Sought to forget unrest in open speech:
"I know not, Annas, I who never feared,
Why I should tremble now when no cause is
Of trembling visible; haply this Christ
Is seen too fearless not to move my fear;
There is a virtue in these stable souls
To cool our wrath to terror. Annas, you,
How like a rock you stood this night, unpropped
Of aught but native during! How unmoved
Amidst commotion, by mere passive front
Reversing peril on its movers! Whence
Have you this mettle?"

Annas, unseduced
By praise, but to the man by fellowship
Moved, in whose purposes he found his own
Described in worthy counterfeit, alone
Of all his peers, replied to him: "My son,
Each man is made by his philosophy.
The care of retribution after death
And dim foreboding of the wrath divine
By the deed merited, though conjectural
And suspect rather than believed, has force
To render man timid to use his life,
To seize care-free the bounty of the earth
By fortune given in hand. So, it is plain,
Fear of the after-life thwarts human ends,
Unsteadies the brave hand in act to grasp,
And cheats men of occasion and at last
Of the ripe fruit of life that autumn-flushed
Too vainly woos their lips. Is not the life
Of those that lack the valor to embrace
In full its content like the life of beasts
Or half-sensed myth of slumber? I have made
Full contract with my mind to live my life
As if the grave closed all, to gather fast
The sure of here and now, nor to take thought
And fumble in the essay, nor to stale
The after-glory with regret. To-night
Defense of office urges; count it fast
That now our foe is fettered; only want
For full immunity the mob's assent
And the death-sentence of the Governor.
The folk are ours; they are but sheep who take

Direction from their shepherds, who prescribe
Desire to them and thought. But for the rest
This Pilate airs his justice and has done
Manfully in his function; therewithal
He has some yielding in him, is not hard
Clean to the heart, as is his iron race
And I am; there lies promise, but time veils
Inexorably the fruit. How leaden now
The minutes of inaction drag their feet!
Caiaphas, I who tremble at no deed
Am half unmanned by deedless calm, for then
Thought becomes clamorous and genius loosed
Corrupts the loyal will. Let us delay
But briefly here, then importunity
Stifle in forthright act!"

                          Silent they stood
And listened while upon the city skirts
The hoarse alarum of the pursuivants
Died to a murmur; from the shaded garth
A rose with Sharon's spices vernal-sweet
Breathed warm fragrance, and the fountain fall
Flashed silver in the moon and uttered chimes
Of mellow laughter in the pool. But they
Projected winter from their angry hearts
Upon the jocund vigil of the spring
And slew the infant summer in her bed,
Till to their eyes nature grew frore and nude
And lifeless; and, forgetful of the prime,
They drew their mantles close and went within.

THERE IS a garden in Gethsemane
Sacred to its own vigil and the touch
Of the immortal feet that never come.
There hushed is all the brawling of the winds
Nor ever shadow stirs save with the pace
Of dialhands that pause when they are viewed;
And noon burns on unshaken, while the stars
Resume the steady torch and the rapt air
Waits breathless for the whisper still withheld.
But through the garden's ancient tombs there drifts
Hint of the everlasting secret, strange
To minds aware, and in her briery chair
Fearless the wild rose cons the farthest light,
Listening. In that lost glade the noded fern
And all the mooning trees and writhed crags
Lie sunk in centuries of ecstasy
So mortal that less rustle is to hear
Than when the questing moth ruffles the haze
Of heat upon a slumbrous summer's noon,

27

Drawn by the white light of the lily-cup,
And settles with a sigh of downy vans
To bathe voluptuous antennae deep
Within the anther and its golden dust,
Infatuate with fire. Far from that haunt
The men of natural hue whose thoughts are lent
To mart or common highroad walk askance
In fear or heedless.

     To that stricken wood
Came our defender strong, the Son of God,
On that predestined eve when he must fight
The field of all the world, alone, self-doomed,
Self-sacrificed. And as he silent stood
Beneath the cold moon in the glade the hate
Of Israel's rulers and the treachery
Of Judas wrung him, but extorted prayer
None but for heavier torment; this he sought,
And the Almighty said "Let it be Fear!"
So to the three of predilection he
Turning bade tarry, and with eager steps
Made toward a grot delved in the knotted rock
Of the hill-steep, where jags of basalt crouched
In adamantine vigil unreprieved
From the world's prime, forbidding sentinels,
Whose feet amid the mounded drift were hid
With mossy runners and tall darnels lithe,
Drooping their seeds in frozen fountains pale
Under the dewfall; and the lintel stone
Beetled with tendrils intricately wove
Of bryony and ivy, whose limp shreds
Swung in the yawning mouth. As he went in

Silence drew close as if with question charged,
But all was dumb, and moveless hung the leaf.

Then fell on him that agony divine.
(O Father, who did smite with sudden bolt
Osa for laying unreflective hand
Upon the sacred ark when David king
And all his men with song and proud refrain
Of timbrel, joyous pipe, and corded harp
Bore it from Gabaa, now be not in wrath
That from his anguished soul I pluck the web
Who is God's more than dwelling-place!) Arose
Before the mind of Christ a hideous form
Contracted not to shape but intimately
In horrid essence grasped, Sin, now at last
Upon the utter righteousness of God
Commanding access. He, impregnable
In absolute being to the attack of pain,
Appareled now in vulnerable flesh
Remembered sin and suffered. He beheld
With mind enthralled, though terrified and wrung,
The universe of that malevolence
That raised war in creation, and in that,
As in a single form, the sins of each,
And time now imminent when the form should cling
To all the avenues of sense and thought
And cloud the evidence of human good.

And as incarnate God, eternal Love,
The inviolable Good, confronted fast
His only adversary, fixed to bar

That self-bestowal which is love in act,
The nature of high good, conflict supreme
Was joined, ideal of all woeful wars,
Exceeding all, between the whole of right
And all its contrary. Beneath its stress
The soul of Christ longed to desert the flesh
That gave him to such onslaught; yet desert
He would not nor forget the thought of sin,
Lest he should purchase dear immunity
From the one thing he dreaded, and dispel
Fear from his sum of torment. Thus began
The bearing of the sins of all the world:
To know essential sin and that his throes,
Extant from the mere knowledge of its act,
Were to atone. No Muse that visits man
Can tell the torments of the Son of God,
Nor all the annals of the fell campaigns
Of earth can feign their terror. These three hours
Did counterfeit eternity by sin
Immutably in the embrace of thought
Locked with Christ's mind in sojourn voluntary
Withdrawn from other musings. Three long hours
In frozen and equivalent debate,
In moveless duel of unyielding foes,
Two hostile forms, the good and rebel ill,
Two powers resolved, each fixed not to prevail
Against the opposing will, nor to submit
By reason of his own, nor to escape
From the engagement by the will of Christ,
Face against face gazed steady and recoiled
In hatred, yet forever gazed and stood.

And in the horror of that rigid strife
Implacable and fear by resolute will
With violence encountered, as time lapsed
The fountains of Christ's blood fused with his sweat,
And all his body trembled, and aloud
He groaned and sank. But, on his couch of blood
Felled with the forces of his manhood drained,
Unfelled, unshaken stood his constant will
Sinless in face of sin, still undeterred
From his elected doom, and from his lips
Pealed victory in words that frighted fear:
"Father, I drink this chalice of all pain;
Your will be done!"
                                Twice in those galling hours
He came to seek the solace of his grief
In sympathy, that unacknowledged praise;
But three hearts smit with presage had recoiled
On sleep, sole refuge from the threat of time,
Heedless of his great need. Then as he sought
Once more the grot of supplication, straight
The face of God, which fed him with delight
Above all possible pain, no longer shed
Its radiance; his memory seemed thrust
Clean from the mind of things, as on his head
Heaven and earth had locked their iron floors
To leave him groping in unpeopled glooms
Below all zones of being, lost in wastes
Beyond the confines of wide-wandering thought.

But on the steep of heaven Gabriel
Chafed to appease his woe, and at the word

Of God stooped on the void with arching breast
And urgent wings distent, then lightly sprang
Sheer from the zenith. In the shadowy glade
The air was moved with rumor of his flight,
Stirred as his lucid vesture shook the air
In thundering swirls behind him. At the grot
He on the bossy summits of the rocks
Sank like a gleaming cloud, and with one hand
Put back the flicker of his wind-combed locks
From hot eyes, fierce and tender. So he stood
Once more before his lord, and low he spoke:

"If there were tears in heaven or if heart
Angelic showed its pity humanwise
Then the eternal day with sore lament
For you, its self-dethroned, self-conquered prince,
Were burdened loud and long. Empty your throne
Where none from the immortal hosts of light
Is worthy to ascend, but in our minds
You reign remembered (I but speak your thought
That sense may echo what the spirit knows).
Not as to outward form but as to act
Of the free mind is honor; and so thrice
Your honor is in heaven, who shall die
Defenseless but unconquered, first as God
The unseducible, as warrior then
Of God the most heroic, third as man
Of men the strongest; to you, mightier man,
The spirits of the Throne obedience vow
And now already mourn your hastening doom
Decreed before all ages to descend

From the sealed watches of this dreadful night.
That doom must come, for wisdom is not free
Nor can dissent from God and yet be wise;
So you, incarnate Wisdom, are constrained
With God to hold your own destruction just
For God's designs, and to desire your fall.
But if not pitiless, not yet in vain
That bitter fall, for evil's reign is checked
And the impious spirits that dared the eternal arms
Chained to their fiery pale. Reason that lights
The eye of man to truth, or, in its sleep,
The blind guide, the divining heart that leads
Infallibly to the last good, shall teach
Multitudes of the office and the state
Of you, the world's desire, and these shall seek
Rather than time's felicity your love.
Full in the highway of the marching years
Your cross shall stand, a challenge to elect,
And shall divide the generations clear
On their eternal ways. But grace, which blunts
The edge of evil purpose, shall endue
Your Church with holiness until your last
Rising and conquest, heavenly Orient,
When in your train the saints, that have pursued
Your steps to Calvary, in raiment clad
Of sun-steeped grain and helms of proudest stars
Revisit this pale day. You eldest-born
Of many Godlike souls, remember now
What trove you gather, when awhile are loosed
The powers of iniquity to rend
Your guiltless flesh, your heart, your self-esteem,

Your whole apparent worth, to furnish forth
A plaything for a night. But fear not time;
Death has no might, Eternal, over you,
Nor on the saints won by your blood, nor yet
Over your Father's changeless love, though veiled
Now to enhance your victory over pain
And render eloquent God's tenderness
To hearts by earth's desires made obdurate;
Time whelms, but the immortal mind abides
With that it covets. Now the fatal hour
Is mantling, and the coverts of the night
Husband strange hatreds. In the secret keep
Of the dark heart intents that fear the sun
Insatiable chafe to fulfil their bent
In naked act, and nature so conspires
To lull man's dread with silence that the wolves
And night-hawks choke amain their boding shrieks;
Only the horns of hell, inaudible
Save to the felon mind, cry on the chase
To you, the wounded deer, alone, betrayed,
To wreak your slaughter; yet your tomb shall break
And vernal, you arise. Now let your shield
Be patience!"
           So the bright archangel spoke,
Then, sped with kindness, sought the unwithering fields.
But Jesus stood, not firmer, but in mind
More quiet, and bent ear to murmur deep
And crackling tresses of the fuming brands
That pressed on through the grove, then with strong pace
Unhurrying sought the three in slumber lost
And roused them unrebuked; "Arise," he said

"For he who will betray me is at hand."
And as they stood he turned with folded hands
Unshrinking, motionless, like some lone tower
Aspiring from a crag, that guards a reach
Of dewy meadows deep and golden shores
Where amber, fragrant from the milky foam
Of flooded tides, is stored; now taciturn,
Of its defenders lorn, its granite pride
Tokens such ire that the beleaguering tribes
Afar stand wary, trailing their feeble spears
In dread surmise.
    So stood the Son of God
Before his foes and all their weapons cruel;
They from the wildwood breaking shouted loud
With triumph of the capture and hard urged
The feet, that with the devious search had lagged,
Forward to apprehend. But, as their last
Broached on the clearing, died the swelling din
Save where the brands with flame invisible
Against the dazzling pallor of the moon
Roared as with inward life. Now hung the horde
With faces livid in the double glow,
Peopling the gazing grove with Parian forms
Moveless and dumb, as if their marble veins
Rose not with blood but stone impermeable,
Stubborn with terror at the unflinching eyes
That saw their souls and froze. Judas alone,
Oblivious of his soul, took no new awe
But other boldness from his band's dismay,
And weakly lusted to be first of men,
Great though in evil, who of old was used

To brook, for felt demerits, their disdain.
So in the face of fear, by use become
Debatable, he, with metallic smile
And meditated gait of ease whose steps
Infirm bewrayed the quaking will that drove,
Drew nigh to Jesus; then, with triumph veiled,
Dissimulated vengeance as he cried
"Hail, Master!" and his venal lips pressed fierce
Upon the harrowed cheek. But as he felt
Beneath his touch rigid and cold the flesh,
Unshrinking but unwelcoming, he knew
Inflexible the spirit of his judge.
He heard the words of grief, "Judas, then thus
Will you betray me?" and with sudden sight
Discerned how an intention in a kiss
Had called the wrath of God on all the earth
And pledged the state of man. Then multiplied
Dread seized him and, with eyes on Jesus' eyes,
Blind to their pleading, for by custom blind,
Backward and ever backward slow he stepped,
Till crumbled resolution to sustain
Their waxing light of doom; then swift he swung
And headlong fled to sanctuary vain
Among the ruthless trees.
                              Still quiet-handed
Asked them the Lord in tone composed and stern
"Whom seek you?" And as who, wafted in sleep
To devious seas, unvisited and cruel,
From the fantastic house of memory
Where self dwells and familiar coasts far lured
By demons from the darkness of the mind,

With ghostly and improper voices speak,
They murmured "Jesus of Nazareth," nor knew
But dimly their own words. And he replied
"I am he," but a beam of power sped
Forth from his Godhead at the words and hurled
Their bodies to the earth. And like a force
Massacred on a stricken field they lay,
Singly or in mutual cumbrance piled,
Twitching their witless and unpurposed limbs,
Bemused with the inevitable. He
Again said "Whom seek you?" And risen some
Again replied "Jesus of Nazareth";
And he said "I have told you I am he;
Let these depart." Then slowly moved few guards
And circumspectly; but the disciples cried
"Lord, shall we strike?" And ere an answer came
Sprang Peter with his short sword and the first
Down smote fierce as Cuchulain when he shone
In orbits of his planetary blade
Alone, undaunted, against multitudes
Guarding the sacred North. But Jesus touched
His fallen foe and healed; to Peter then:
"Put up your sword, O undiscerning! Now
My conquest is by sacrifice. Know you
I have ten thousand legions at my beck,
My Father's household?" Upward glanced his eye
To where the hosting of the seraphim
Made lunar twilight; Michael and his host
In splendor terrible, more terrible
In anger now, made prayer to get command
To sear the impious earth with flaming glaives,

Make havoc of man's works, and scorch to dust
His small presumptuous flesh; and from the verge
Of the horizon to the utmost pole
Blotting the stars, but few and wan beside,
Squadrons of spirits swept or hovered dire
With swords athirst for the blasphemers' lives.
But he invoked them not, and to the mob
Turning he said: "Why come you out thus armed
As to a thief to me whose peace you know?
For in the temple daily I have been
Yours to endure your will."
                              But they awoke
At his inaction from the stupor cast
By sense of might unearthly, and recalled
At that one artless blow their mazy minds
To the reports of sense and unresource
Apparent of their foe. So to his words
They made no answer but, unanimous
In rage more rabid grown by memory
Of the late spell of fear flung by his scorn,
They fell on him. And all the multitude
Shouted with strange, unmeaning utterance,
And all engaged to handle undismayed
With numerous clutch his members, and to spy
Upon his face the passions of the mind
That felt its future torments in its fear;
And on each arm four soldiers heedless hung
That it was quick with sense, until the clash
Of combats, objurgations, and debates
Confounded night. Alone of all who strove
Jesus was master of his deeds, and limp

And unresisting to their onset swayed,
Nor cried, nor yielded from his eyes content
Nor from his face its calm, but took the grasp
That each with surfeit of endeavor pressed
As one inviting. So with uproar huge
Fast corded they his passive wrists and swung
The thong around his body and before
Tied for a leading-string; then, wheeling face,
The unretrospective and unheeding guards
Towed him, their conqueror, while tedded far
Through the wild burrs hastened the throng ahead
To turn and look behind and meet his eyes
And taste vicarious anguish. So they groped
Down to the leafless hollow and defiled
Through the dry-throated narrow of the hills
Where passed the sanded causeway; and in time
Traversed the bridge where from the mountains fell
The torrent Kedron, meditating song
To its own ears, but deaf to every speech
Beyond the syllables of self to self,
Prisoner of its own being. Upward thence
They found the track that flanked the pendent scarp
Of the vast precipice whose mailed thighs
Bastioned the sacred city, and at last
They spurned the topmost brink and took on high
The wind chill on their cheeks, and from the abyss
Below them, dim in the sheeted glare of the moon,
Turned. Then beneath the splendor of the fane
Of God they marched in sullen disarray,
Where with supernal pride the needled towers
Uttered blanched lightnings to the taunting stars

And brandished their indented architraves
Against the reeling rack. Here veered the troop
Round to the southern gates.

                             But far behind
The followers of Jesus fled away
Despairing; only John and Peter turned
And clung the rear confounded; and one more
Disdained to flee but pressed the steps of Christ,
Wild boy unclad but for his linen zone,
Taking the moonlight with his blown red hair.
But came a soldier and to bar him grasped
The zone and tore it from him; timid he
Into the shrubs dived lightly and at once
Quenched his white limbs in darkness.

                                And all these
Passed from the boding silence into pain.
But Judas in the vale of agony
Stole from the briers, and upon the gleam
Of the receding escort looked in dread,
And said within his heart: "Must it then be
That ever the elected ill appears
The greater at its imminence? No, no,
The uncorrupted mind that counsels choice
Approves it ever, and with constant act
Vindicates it in adverse consequence;
But now the truth revealed reveals the ill
Incurred more monstrous than the ill surmised
And chosen, and too late disowns the choice.
This hour have I beheld might measureless
To fill my hands with wealth and my desires
Shine in the eyes of Christ, or yet to damn

Beyond all hope in anguish infinite;
And they have damned me. O, no sentence else
Was carried in their reprobative thrust
But power and the will to damn with it;
Those eyes were estimates of coming doom,
Earned for improvidence. Now must I save
The life within their deeps or contemplate
Their mockery for my eternal days.
Time drives to deed then, ere the issue find
Its term, and me to long destruction pledge;
Now to undo my work or be undone!"
Musing he stood and strengthened his resolve
Looking aloft. A wedge of wild duck blurred
Swiftly the silver kirtle of a cloud,
But to his fearful fantasy they seemed
Tall characters of wrath by hand unseen
Limned on the heavens, chronicling his days,
A curse imperishable. Then, firm with dread
The last joist to uphold of sloping self,
He sought Mount Sion and the sacred walls
To turn the counsels of the Sanhedrin.

BOOK

THREE

ONCE MORE I supplicate your secret voice,
Immortal Muse, not of the nine who rose
When man first knew inexorable need
Of heaven and begot it with his mind,
But you whom at the prelude of my song
I sought for guide, the principle of minds
And of all truth to them, the heaven desired
That was before its knowledge. Breathe on me,
O Joy of Truth in its own changeless Fair,
Which is subsistent Song, from whom descend
Tidings unearthly and great comforting
To man through lips prophetic, when you will,
Lord, to illuminate our mortal dusk
With gift of knowledge inaccessible
Or stir with strain of your ethereal song
The mind devout to music. You long since
Brimmed the cupped ear upon the Patmian rock
Of the forsaken seer with gospel, borne
On airy symphonies of hollow tones

From golden-throated horns, delighting him
With tidings of the bridal of the bride,
God's hidden truth in trust, with music clad
Such as to light man's knowledge through his ears.
Be you sole doctor of my reason now,
Exiled from men by this oblivion
Of all but you; nor teach me truth concealed
To man prohibited, I ask, but aid
The natural wit to know what can alone
Its intellectual valor. Smite my tongue
With Pentecostal virtue that it speak
The polyglot of hearts; for now the tryst
Now when contend proud man and abject God,
Created god and the creator God,
Ward of all keys save to the franchised will,
The right and rebel at the heart of things,
Unconquered earth and heaven unconquerable,
But earth in panoply and heaven forsworn,
Who will not and who cannot yield. Conduct
My mind to read the warring motives right,
Judgments inconstant and divergent ends
Of all who wrought in the Redeemer's woe,
That in their conflicts may appear to me
The unity of your design imposed
By purpose first and last; set me in sight
The will in act to order and instruct
Of the divinity in the event,
That I may sing your universal arm,
The One from whom the many have begun,
To whose intent blindly their deeds conspire,
Though wrought to thwart you, Providence supreme,

Haven of this self-persecuted world.

Now Annas at the crisis of the world
Watched with the purpose in his will confirmed
That in the plan of God was to procure
Eternal life or death to every man.
But he, to the eternal issue blind,
Held fast in thought only his instant aim
And fixed intent, hateless and pitiless,
Freedom to win, the matter of all power,
By shattering the traverse to his will
And reign by slaying. In a chamber laid
For calm deliberation he sat on,
One hand clutching the high boss of his chair,
And one the thickets of his beard, and all
His consciousness demanding the report
Of Christ's detention. Rigid stood his thralls
Around him and with unuplifted eyes
Acknowledged him by terror and their minds
Intent upon his nod. Thus all of them,
Made numb by expectation, stood at gaze
Like monuments, their whole souls in their ears.

At last the leaden silence stirred afar
With premonition, and the listeners
Started like runners to their poising toes
With eager eyes bright-raised to the dim port
Where moaned the pregnant night. And presently
They saw the minions of the pontiffs there
And in their midst was Jesus in his bonds;
But as they were at hand they made great show,

With threat and toil obsequious, of zeal
To him whose cause those urged, and hastily
Impelled their captive into the pale glow
Of silver lamps around the single chair,
And, spent with their achievement, strenuously
Stood still and waited for their dole of praise.
But Annas knew only the respite sweet
Of feared disaster, savoring curiously
With the fantastic palate victory
And the occasion won to have his will
Of his great enemy. So triumphed he
A space in silence, then in accents cold
He charged him peremptory:
                          "Ill augurs it
That you, O overweening, dare to this
Our absolute regency, for now revolt
Is out and you must bide its punishment
As we will; now your single might is gyved,
And all the furious smoke of popular love
Snuffed at our sovereign word, and you will come
Soon to the bound of life. Only remains
Mercy to win by feeding ignorance;
For we, who dedicate us to the good
Of those we rule, are too indifferent
To pain within us to have lust to quench
In torment of another, too removed
From fear to covet terror in our foes.
Instruct me on your doctrine then and aim,
And you shall find the passage to your death
A painless passage to the end of pain.
Come, if you are as brave and wise as famed,

Endure with peace inevitable grief
But be not eager grief to aggravate;
It is becoming wisdom's loyalist
To forfeit but with need."

                              Thus he conjured
And, while he spoke, regarded his intent
Lest some unheeded motive should distort
The fitness of the act deliberate
For present circumstance and purpose fixed
By judgment. Yet escaped his scrutiny
A master dread that swayed his inmost self,
Unknown to him, for he disdained to know,
Lest in Christ's mind his mien of majesty
In peril should betray knowledge of power
Secret and inconceivable. So fear,
Offspring of mystery, acknowledged not,
Softly its credited supremacy
Stole from the watching mind, and to the words
Malign of Annas lent a friendly mask
To lure from Christ confession not of guilt
But of his hidden subsidy. But he
Replied and with his candor baffled him:
"All days to all men I have told the truth
Openly in the temple, and by stealth
No single truth. Why ask what all men know?"
And straight another torment he of God
Sought, and was given shame.

                              For one stood by
Who wooed his master's favor, and with eyes
Turned to the face of Annas now he smote
Full with his hand the lips of Christ and cried

"Is such your speech to the high priest?" But Christ
Answered "If I have spoken any ill
Declare it, but if well why strike you me?"
And Annas raged at the untimely blow
And rose and shouted "Back, churls, I will speak
Of things unfitting for the ears of slaves."
And as they drew into the confines dim
Of the resounding chamber he sank back
Upon the chair and for an instant sensed
The question of a hundred unseen eyes,
Unfriendly witnesses that in the light
Cloaked their hearts' freedom by obeisance feigned.
So to defeat their eager ears he leaned
Forward to Christ and, honoring him, spoke
These to him low:
                        "I am what I desire,
As each man is the process of his end
Striving with adverse chance and you of men
Are but the thing you love in the degree
Of your achievement of your heart's design;
Our self-perfection only then is foiled
When one would be what would another be
And emulation tangles both. O Christ,
Twin genius to my own and fellow heir
To rulership by your like mind declared,
This age is ours or it we must dispute
With all its wealth and all the loyalties
Of smaller men, private or privileged;
For nature that has given us our powers
Has made us rectors of the coming time
Most patently, or has decreed to one

His death. You and I are too great for faith,
By willing and achieving make our truth
And flout the auguries. Perhaps the truth
That you would be I would not, and to slay
You is to maim myself, so to declare
The terms of coexistence needs but we
Declare our fixed intents. Nature or God
Has made me kingly; since the break of thought
Destroyed my childhood I have known myself
Displaced when one above me is to spurn
My brow with insolent heel; and I have schemed
As privily as yet relentlessly
By overthrow of all that stood between
To be the first of men. Melancholy,
Both child and foe of future toil foreseen,
Like all who would accomplish I have cast,
Telling my heart I had eternal years
To win the kingdom lost to me awhile
Yet ever destined in my nature. Nay,
I cannot think how I, ambition's jade,
Shall stay the stab of the harsh rider's spur
Till I have vailed the fearful spears of Rome
And chained her kings to my imperial wrist
Fast as the earth has yoked and swung the spheres
And flung to them their laws. Since this my bent,
Think not that I can brook your fellowship,
Who scarce brook God's; but if you can constrain
Your prowess to be vassal but of mine
And lord of the great throng of lesser men
We may atone us. Wherefore loose your mind,
By nature frank, that we may strike the points

Of composition. Think not to avoid
For I can wring your soul. I stand not by
The wordy Plato sworn that all men seek
The one good excellent beyond defect;
For the complexions of our elements,
Various as the conjunctures of our stars,
Must fix us varied ends, and for event
Particular goods endue the absolute
For our particular minds. Give me but sign
Of the one tyrant passion in a man
Drawing his life as lode-star or as god,
Be it the love of woman or of wealth,
Or thirst unquenchable for knowledge hid,
Or fixed ambition, the divine disease,
Or zest for sounding deeds, and I shall press
Him to my will by offer of his own
Or threat to bar its seeking, past all power
To shirk the goad. Nor think you yet to clothe
Your bosom in a proof of silence, thus
Embattled fast in your autonomous will
To taunt attempt; freedom is impotent
To flee the probe of pain, nor lies in man
To face the imminence of full surcease,
Made sensible while sensibly his soul
Slides from his groaning members, and to gripe
Liefer his proposition than the pledge
Of respite of the end. I love you not
Nor pity, and my purpose is confirmed,
Inevitably prescribed as prophecy,
To wrest you to my will or to destroy.
I, patient as the spider fixed at gaze

All day, while scarcely creeps the laboring sun,
Near to his cunning threads, have wove my toils
To clog the Roman eagles, and as calm
Can watch you faint therein, while I invoke
Engines of torment, prudent counselors
Of changed resolve, to conjure up strange fears,
Patrol with hideous claws flesh imbecile,
In slow deliberate series burst each bone,
Obstruct the healing rites of nature, fill
The train of the ambassadors of death,
By which their lord himself and I effect
The articles of your transfer, one by one,
In calculated contract. Only you
Can foil negotiation at the price
Of candid speech. Come, though all men be false
I cannot think that you are!"
      So he spoke
The truth unmeditated to his end.
But straight a breath inspired the flame which swept
Across the face of Christ and bared the eyes
Steadfast, uneager, and unterrified.
And Annas started backward as now first
Terror, the ape of failure, touched his sense;
A moment still he gazed, then swiftly drew
His strength to resolution and stood up
And raised his angry voice: "Ho, guards, to me!
Your high priest is contemned! Handle and lead
Straight to the Sanhedrin!" Upon the word
They sprang from the deep gloom and with their hands
Grappled Christ's shoulders, then with single wheel
Unanimous they bore him through the porch

Dividing the dense night. But Annas sat
Alone in the vast chamber, suddenly
Aware of time and glory unachieved
And doom at hand to scatter his few gains
And all his hope; a moment he was old
And shattered, then, self-spurred at sudden thought
His valor rose to foil the envious years
And with new face of hate and leveled glance
He strode to his allies.

                Meanwhile took Christ
The pang of solitude. Peter and John,
Like dumb, impetuous moths that prosecute
Blindly their ruin in a dying flame,
Followed afar the last of the wide throng
Convoying Jesus. But their steps were slow,
For love which drove was cumbered with despair;
And as the night with press of darkness swooped
Down from the soaring walls, and they by all
Were distanced, then their fear interpreted
Silence as menace and to greatness fed
On its own creature. But, though faltering,
Fighting they sought their lord, till once again
The murmur and the gleam of earth informed
The chaos of the night, and close at hand
They saw dim in the air a gate of dark
That upward flung its columns till immersed
In the abyss of gloom they seemed to sweep
The heavens with their arch; its avenue
Was with two lions of bright granite flanked,
That gazed with void and unimpassioned eyes
Forever beyond time. Here traversed John

The pontiffs' threshold with assured mien
And unalarmed eyes, but hostile chance
Held Peter, as upon the selfsame quest
Of him who is the riches of the Grail,
Of which the Blest Age sang, the knights were foiled
At many a torrent or enchanted keep
Or monster of a race long since consumed.

There was an ancient portress in the gate
Long dwelling, who had nourished through her life
Her one desire for tidings of the strange
By questioning all passers; feeble now
Her mind still urged to question, though inept
To take the answer's pith. So wondered she
At Peter's anxious mien, and him surmised
With groping argument foe to her lord,
And probed him thus, though to the purpose sole
Of knowing: "Stay, you moody man of haste,
Are you not of the followers of Christ?"
But he, with all his mind fixed on one care,
Intolerant of any thought but that,
Seized the first way to quench her prying bent
And answered all but heedless: "No, make way!"
And speaking he strode on and crushed the fear
That he had Christ forsworn with praise of self
And memory of the hour when he alone
Had smitten for the Lord.
                              And so he stood
Within the close with its tall columns hemmed
That branched in many arches and were still,
Like to those groves of blackest burgeon where

The bloody rites of the Phoenician gods
Darkened the lunar noon. So Peter stood
And felt himself with evil circumscribed,
Viewed by all vagrant eyes, and to prevent
The queries that the isolated start
He sought the frequent brazier. In the throng
He sat with listless finger-twined hands
Folding one knee, and, fearful to show fear,
With foolish smile of simulated ease
Trembling he looked whereso no eye sought his.
Betimes, on mischief bent, there came a maid,
Armed with the fatal grace of youth, and kneeled
And leaned in studied pose of negligence
Her hair flame-snooded on the knuckles gnarled
Of Peter while the lambent light caressed
Her kerchief's dainty disarray. His pulse
More highly beat as she with laughing eyes
Sought his and with her piping voice, devised
To bind her moment's conquest, questioned him:
"Are not you too a Nazarene?" But he
Was loth to mend his perfidy by words
Denying those late uttered and the debt
To cancel them confessing to his mind,
Lest he should self-convicted stand and quit
The comfortable sense of undefect,
The fabricated credence that conceals
The fugitive, who knows the truth and dreads,
From the pursuit of self. So "Damsel" he
Replied with heat as of the just man wronged
"You prattle nonsense!" and he straight arose
And sought a place apart and other ears.

But some that heard followed with stern intent
To probe the matter, others but to gain
Brief respite from the prison of their cares
In others' passion; and the various mob
Of the dishevelled soldiery, and slaves,
Scullions and menial ministers of the spit,
In stinking clouts, with rabid eyes of threat
Or cruel glee, swarmed around Peter, loud
With question of his Galilean speech,
Or witnessing that he had struck the blow
That drew blood in the garden. And to him
It seemed that forms of stature more than man's
Were hosting for his sacrifice, and stood
In congregated thousands over him,
Bowing in turn toward him their livid brows
To cry the tidings of preparing doom
Into his frenzied ears, should he affirm.
As the Dedannan warlocks on the beach
Of fairy Carnsore by enchantments damned
Fretted the demon spirits of the flood
To heave the waters of the sullen sea
To serried mountains, which with horrent crests
Of hissing slaver and concave bellies pinched
Bore down on the invading ships and gulped
The whole Milesian host; so to the eyes
Of Peter menaced now the household churls
Of Annas, and, distraught with ecstasy
Of fear, he scorned his lord, unsaid his pride:
"I struck no blow; I am no friend to Christ."
Forthwith the fatal cock unloosed the paean
That wakes pale Lucifer to lead the morn

Out of the downy east; and from the gate
Of Annas, Christ was guided by strong hands,
Who, as he passed, lifted his eyes a flash
And joined with Peter's, tranquil witnesses
Of unimpassioned knowledge. Peter there
Discerned the truth that he had now forsworn,
And at the objurgation of his heart
He hated that which he had bought, his life,
And wept, and beat his brow, and went from thence.

But now the session of the Sanhedrin
Gathered again in the great hall of doom,
Where in the boundless darkness the red brands
Maintained an isle of fire, the only gleam
Won from the usurpation of the night
Save where, between the shadowy columns far,
Silent and dim the stars peered pendulous.
There sat the lords of the tribunal, proud
And still as stone gods of a savage eld,
In two wide horns, dumb with insistent care;
And high in the rear mists a kingly seat
Loomed dimly and with menace visible
Empty foretold its sitters, the supreme
Controllers of the Synod. To that tryst
Of midnight all had come that in the light
Had plotted save Gamaliel the Just,
Who feared to see weak and in bonds a man
Whom he had hoped divine, and solitary
Now nourished on the hope feigned by desire
His hopeless heart.

Into that rapt precinct
Came clamor loud and then the Son of God
Beaten and bound amid his captor crew,
Nor there had any sense of fellowship
For fear had stopped their pity at its springs.
Then like a demon from the coasts of Dis
Kindling to life that rigid company
By flame of his own passionate intent
To have his vengeance, Annas swept, and fast
Behind him Caiaphas. And all the throng
Were troubled into thought by pressing deeds,
And shook with comment and conjecture dim
Of contest pending; but the purposed team
Wordless ascended to the lofty throne
Where Annas softly spoke to Caiaphas:

"It must be absolute. The man must die,
As you yourself have said, to save our church.
For if the downward pressure of grave Rome
Were met with warfare of the inward parts
All would dissolve; his death will check dissent
And give us respite; now we jeopard all
If this same hour we find not cause to slay.
He has required we seek his teaching's proof
In those that heard him; he shall have his will
And sign that he has taught to ours. Now call
The witnesses that you have tutored; if
Their schooling prove defective, I still keep
One sleight he shall not slip with all his wit.
Despatch the cause!"

Thus Annas, and took seat.
But Caiaphas stood up and charged the court,
Irked by the need to weigh a fearful choice:
"My lords, this hour must judge the church of God:
This man with breeding treason manifold
Is taxed, and you shall hear the kinds forthwith;
If the false charge be patent then secure
We loose the captive, but should we detect
Some semblance of the truth in those who plead
Then loose we at our peril. This same night
Must see our action perfect or our power
Offered to bonds. Let the accuser speak,
And innocent blood recoil upon his head!
But should he shield the guilty, then God's wrath
Shall strike him for the ruin of his race."

Then stood the accuser forth at Jesus' side.
He was the same who at the abhorred gate
Of Magdala among the leper band
Had languished many years, until alone
Accosted he the Lord upon his way
Who rinsed him from his scabs. And thankless he
Departed; but the debt of gratitude
Weighed him till he interpreted with hate
Its burden as a chain by Jesus wrought.
And to escape its question he contrived
To see ill-purpose in the words and deeds
Of his repairer. Now he stood to plead
His justice to the priests, most to himself,
And so began:

"That I am saved by you
From blind submission to the Nazarene,
I thank you, sirs; that I am called to aid
In his erasure from the wholesome day,
I thank you, sirs, again; that I am healed
Of canker foul which most iniquitous chance
Shriveled my innocent flesh and bone withal,
I thank not him, who made to vegetate
And by infernal simples bloomed my cheeks
For his obscure designs. I were suborned
Did the well-being of my single flesh
Now seal my silence when my speech could stop
The grief of Israel. Hear then: He said
To these my ears, while trembled I to hear:
'Your fathers eat of manna and are dead,
But he who eats the bread that is my flesh
Will never die,' as who should say in brief:
'I am the true and mighty God, but they
Worshiped one impotent who gave them food
Of no avail against death's instancy';
And added to make favor with the scribes
Attendant, such things of the antique use
Of our forefathers in the cult of God
As to make suspect that their liturgy
But wasted all the reek of sacrifice
Upon an empty idol of the mind,
More unsubstantial than a graven stock."

But Caiaphas cried out "It is enough,"
And saw with fear the face of Annas frown,
"Require a witness."

           Then stood Banther forth,
Banther, the lover of the Magdalen,
Who for the feet of Christ left his embrace
And him with rage on fire. Triumphant now
He stood and laughed on Jesus, listening mute,
Then spoke to Caiaphas: "O, be assured,
You have a devil; thoughts he has confessed
That brim the sum of possibility
Of evil will to breed. These have I heard,
And whatsoever perfidy, my lords,
You please to lay on him that can I found
On witness of my faithful sense." To him
Caiaphas made quick question: "Heard you him
Advocate new observance and condemn
The worship of our forefathers?" But he:
"Nay more; for you, doctors of Israel,
He charged with hiding from the use of men
The key of knowledge of the ancient law
And heresy by ignorance imposed
Upon our sires' fidelity."
                    But straight
One stood, prompted by terror lest the scheme
Should snare the schemers, and on Caiaphas
Cried out: "Unskilled avenger, Caiaphas,
Improvident victim of your instruments,
Now must you find more trusty tools of fraud
If you would have our hands with yours. We, forced
To break the law here in the law's defense,
Abide the peril of the wrath of God,
But to inevitable punishment
As well from man we are not pledged. Inept,

These witnesses conflict and full report
Will din the ears of Israel and Rome
To our undoing: either we dismiss
The traitor to let loose his subtle strength
Against our harried race, or warrant death
By the deeds sworn unwarranted; no proof
Of malice that will move the Roman sword
Or satisfy of justice Israel
Can we declare; destruction guards each way,
And one man's folly has dissolved the state."

So he in anger and bewilderment.
But Annas with grave aspect and smooth speech
Arose unbidden and replied: "Perverse
Are you to charge him, friend, with artifice
And purchased testimony, though crisis oft
And present threat frame their own law and right.
Nor is there conflict in the testimony,
For he who sets himself in place of God
Must yet resent the disobedience
To God that he divines; for it denies
His own claims with the rights of God on man.
Nay, though diverse their testimony, these men,
Ingenuous and at one in bitterness
Against the captive, found surmise of guilt;
And, do we press the quest, doubt not the truth
That even now reveals to us its head
Will bear it hideous to our penal sword.
We were more shamed to hazard Israel
Than to destroy one man for treachery,
Not to the skeptic mind of advocacy

But to the presage of the sedulous heart
All but declared. Wherefore now, Caiaphas,
Bid other witnesses!"
     So next there came
At call of Caiaphas a starving one
Mindful alone of food, and so the more
Secure to tell by rote unpondering
The ordered lie, and gather his reward.
He with relentless will heeding his words,
Pledges of hope, the while his eyes sought out
Restless the prophecy of alms engraved
Upon the silent faces, loud and swift
Gave tongue nor paused till twice he had renounced
His full tale to its author: "I have heard
His vaunt, that if you should demolish clean
The temple, he could rear it in three days
Upon its rubble."
     But the haughty priest
Waived with auspicious brow his further speech
And called his fellow, glorious of his state
To be the counsel of the Sanhedrin,
Who thus declared: "I in the selfsame hour
Heard his command to level Herod's fane,
And promise to erect within three days
Its fallen towers."
     But the same councilor
That lately had inveighed on Caiaphas,
Made wary by the semblance of deceit
In the first evidence spied, with mind intent
Had weighed word against word to extricate
The dangerous knot of doubt. Now from his seat

Divided he again on sudden thought
And with his question the attestant checked
In his mid utterance: "Promised he, he would,
Or said he but he could? For can and will
Bewray not like intents." But he, dispelled
Straight from his eminence of fantasy
By fear to beard the priest, voiced the first sense
That came and said: "I speak but as I learned
What I was taught"; and fled in sudden fear.

Then turned the questioner on Caiaphas
And spoke in wrath: "O, treachery supreme
That even itself betrays! O Caiaphas,
How have you brought our office to disdain,
And on our heads indignant recompense
Invoked from Rome and from the Jews we rule,
Soon to despoil us of our sway! Accursed
Now be your life before you share with us
Inevitable fall! Since to evade
We have no means, nor one associate
Can summon to our aid; for the brass heaven
Hurls back the prayers of its antagonists,
And hell heeds no petition from its friends.
Confederacy with you has wrought our doom,
And proved the justice of your enemy,
Justice victorious. See him! His eyes
Are steady and his silence is informed
With knowledge unrevealed but damning us.
Now were our hands not with blood coveted
Too soiled to loose his bonds and so his tongue,
I could find will to slay you with my sword

And free the Nazarene; but we must act
To cheat our fate, though no act can avail.
And so, O Caiaphas, take this to mind:
If this destruction seize us, if the Jews
Forego their loyalty for our crimes, and Rome
Manacle our abused authority,
Straight to be noised, it shall be noised therewith
That yours were the decoys, yours the thwart craft,
Yours the misprision of law, and you the first
Of all your tribe shall go to ground, a curse
Undying for all ages while our race
Shall wear its bonds. Find you resource to quench
Our jeopardy or be the first to fall!"

They heard with mounting spleen, but feared perplexed,
Then turned on Caiaphas with single sway
Their dim and wide-eyed faces, multitudes
With question on their fixed and noiseless lips,
Pale as hushed tapers watching round a lyke.
But he stood still and strove with wrath awhile,
Then, yielding to the oversweeping rage,
Swift and inevitable from his place
Strode down, and stood the distance of his arm
From him who seemed the author of his plight.
Closely he peered on him as if intent
To wrest reply from the defiant breast
By main imperative, and with command
Arming his voice cried out: "Are you untongued,
That you to these indictments make no plea?"
Yet Jesus looked with unalarmed will
Into his eyes and held his peace. But soft

Stepping behind came Annas to put curb
On the priest's lawless rage, and caught his robe
And whispered with a deadlier hate of calm:
"Not so shall you prevail; he is too fast.
For I have by surmise explored, by word
Have visited the passes of his mind
Sealed by his stubborn will, and he will yield
Freedom and entry but where law demands.
Only the mind whose destiny is royal
Is its own law and molds all to its will;
His I have probed and find no trend in him
Save to obey what law he finds; such slaves
Of chance are framed for death. Now it is writ
That he whom the High Priest shall charge by God
To answer shall put forth the truth. Do you
Demand in the Lord's name if he pretends
To be the Son of God, and he will yield
To show of right which is pretense of power."

Thus Annas, of the power he must beware
At last apprised, yet ever obdurate
Against avowed assent to the truth feared,
Contrived to move its change. But Caiaphas
With new intention fired turned upon Christ
And cried "I charge you by the living God,
Are you the Son of God?" And Jesus frowned
And spoke:
       "What though the solace of your years
Of labor and the ever-living truth
I show to you, nor solace nor the truth
Will you receive but to be instrument

Of your iniquity. But, since by right
You question, in God's name take my reply:
Even as you say, I am the Son of God
And God by sonship who, for love of men,
Save them by dying at their hands of hate.
Now mischief has its hour and it is yours,
But comes the day when shall my Sire in heaven
The fearful session of the final doom
Invoke on the spent world, and you shall see
Me in the chair of the tribunal placed,
Your judge that day, as you to-day are mine."
They heard compelled, some flinched and were for flight;
But Annas to prevent, with held regard
On Christ, cried swiftly "Blasphemy!" and straight
"Blasphemy!" shouted Caiaphas, "No more
Need we of witnesses!" and ripped his cloak
In feigned lament with vast and horrid noise
From throat to hem, and "Blasphemy!" cried all
And smiled as at the prowess of their cause
Recalled to minds distract with craven care,
"He has earned death." And the thin clamor rose
Of puny exultation through the deep
Embrasure of the universal air
And on the echoes of the vault outborne
Troubled sleep's empire with the name of Death.

But in the center of the alarmed world,
The hall's dim-flickering heart, where first the woe
Was uttered, they contrived to meditate
Their wrath as opposition to a wrong
Which to redress were valiant. And one sprang

And strongly smote the ivory cheek of Christ
Until he reeled; and one to vaunt his scorn
Spat on the swaying raiment, in one act
Spurning his anguished conscience and its lord.
Then with the moment of a cloud of kites
That from the steep of some untenanted peak
Stoop on a maimed eagle, when their first
Is bold to tear the golden quills, more bold
Screaming they plunge for the brave sense of war
On so superb a foe, so the whole throng,
Grown emulous to punish, sudden swept
In onset dire on Christ. Lewd images
Unbidden shaped their guardless speech and broke
From the lips' sanctuary in warring din
Tempestuous; and every hand was raised
To quick the sense of triumph with a blow.
And now the face of Jesus bore assault
Of buffets till the weary strikers paused;
Sealed were the eyes, and sealed the dolorous mouth,
And sealed the murmuring spirit; yielded the veins
Alone their crimson flood, while in the pelt
Of bruises he as anvil to the sledge
Offered himself and staggered at the swinge.
Then as they stood outworn while yet the roar
Invective in the eddies of the night
Rang fevered, stepped a server to his back
And whipped a tattered neckerchief about
The listless eyes, and with a sidelong glance
On his admired despots knocked amain
The sagging head and cried "Predict, O seer
Of far and future, who has stricken you!"

And with their anger turned to glad contempt
Before his silent and defenseless front,
Derisive they with renewed process swooped
Of blows, insulting in their strength discerned.
Still was he silent, still unmoved, and still
The air was jangled with their revelry
Till limbs again were spent, and he who bound
Now with pain satisfied undid the bands.
But Jesus lifted travail-laden lids
And glimpsed with waning eyes his foes' array,
Then to the reasty earth bowed his fair head
And sank all limber as a settling hern
Among its seething plumes.
                                Then solemn all
Towered above him while their glances dire
Fell scalding on his struggling veins, as whist
And rigid as a haggard effigy
Of the spent victors of a fateful field.
But Annas peremptory burst the ring,
And turned and spoke to fan their hardihood
To bloodier height: "O now I see you men,
Nay, conquerors of men with all that rounds
The destined diadem; this body pleads
In you the clean defect of faltering will,
The purple of true sovereignty, the power
To dominate occasion, and to worst
Basilisk fear by challenge to fulfil
Its bruited menace; manfully have you
Unveiled the weakness of the Nazarene
By bold confronting and in the act declared
The falsehood of his claims and what his meed.

But much remains ere we can spy our hopes
Ripen to solid truth, and the fixed will,
Foil of death's sickle and the scythe of time,
Must bend not for the reaping. We must win
Assent of Israel by full rehearse
Of his confession at the right assize
Set public at the city's navel; then
Assent of Rome must follow to his death;
Then Israel will yield and Rome must seek
Assent of us, the suzerains of the Jews—
Kneeling as one to the theocracy
That the Almighty founded in the field
Where life waked the first man—to hold her gains
Or slip them at our word. Imperial
That freedom. O bright star of prophecy
Kindled by no far, crazed antiquity,
But by these wills divine! See, we are fates
And build the future from our skeiny thought,
If we be but intolerant and swift,
Cruel and impatient to perfect the mesh
Of woven purpose. Tarry now no more,
Nay, not to think; new thought will stay your hands.
When you must kill him ere tomorrow's eve
To hold the towers that Machabaeus won;
But be to your old thoughts blind powers at call,
Faithful and instant, murmurless and strong,
As to Jehovah's hand are thunderbolts,
Storms and eclipses, avalanches, plagues,
That slay at his behest, nor know their work
Of pauseless devastation. Now, to act!
Straight let our servants carry him to bide

His waking in a bolted cell, while we
Foregather at the Pontiff's Judgment Seat
To wait the multitude. And may the heavens
Approve what we unfailingly shall wreak!"

So they upraised the throbbing members lax,
That on the pavement groped with swelling life,
On pensioned arms, and in funereal file
With slow, deliberate steps but with high heads,
Lit with the glamor of impassioned hope,
Fanatical resolve, infallible might,
Terrible and august they shadowy flowed
After to the first twilight. But the last,
Annas, stayed Caiaphas with urgent words:
"See how the stars and auspices incline
Fondling upon us! He whom now we rend
Is all compact of virtue; haply none
Of those that mold the fortunes of the mass
Possesses so the conquerable world
By conquest of himself; Caesar in Rome
Is but a vane to him, mounted upon
Inconstant purposes of fonder minds
Whom he has spurned to rise, and governing
By exercise of custom that his dead
And mightier ancestry has shaped. And now,
Whether we win Christ to us or undo,
We can assess ourselves of finer worth
Than Caesar and his peers. I could nigh wish
That he had knit with us, but since his will
Is settled to outvie us it must be
By his destruction. Weigh these words and feed

Your mettle on them! Haste we now to act,
Nor ever fold our wings nor taste sweet rest
Till we have burst this bar."
                                        So he, and both
Followed into the paling night. And soon
Out of the hall's most gloomy nook crept John
Tracing the skirts of dusk to the barren lanes
To weep, to wonder, and to brood inert.

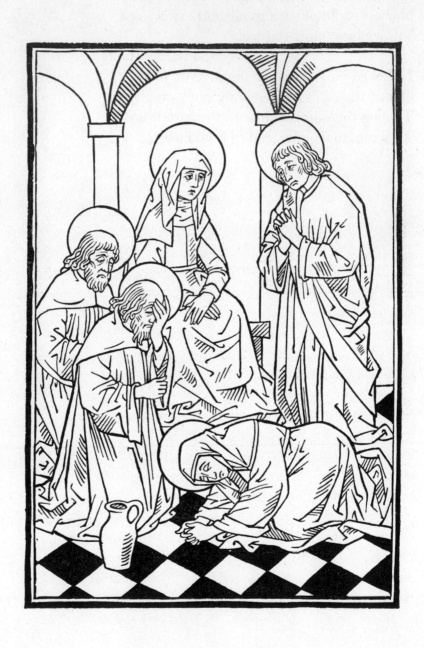

BOOK

FOUR

Now in the east the chill and silver wave
  Of daybreak tided through the drowsed defiles
  And washed the airy turrets with wan stream,
Hardly evoking pale and struggling forms
Charmed from the dewy darkness, and the roofs
Prone of the hallowed city. No eye yet
Saw the cold lotus in the pool's recess
Or in the garth the contemplating rose
Loosen the heavy eyelid; nor marked ear
Faint-thought the birds, whose shrill and tender peals
Follow the foot of morning, fill the air
With a weak clamor. Only the mind drew back
Regretful from the solitary plains
Of sleep and its nocturnal wanderings
To drink alternate rapture from the light
Anadyomene. So with the smothered pain
Of the new birth of waking stirred the earth
And lived again with light. But while the world
Now donned its dewy weeds and waxen snood

73

And joyed in the sweet pang of change and breathed
A passionate life of love to beauty risen
Which stung and calmed, the fellowship of Christ
Knew no return of beauty nor reverse
Of the dominion of imperious night,
But in their hearts usurping melancholy
Sat changeless, and the retrospective dark
Inhabiting endured, breaking their thoughts
In rout disordered and enduing fear,
And sallies of despair, and nerveless doubt,
And boding which is born of ignorance,
Till change itself seemed bliss though change were fell.
Deep in the city's heart there stood a house
To few familiar, where in a dim room
The fugitives of that broken fellowship
Were gathered. There, with spirits marveling
At life persisting with their purpose foiled,
Amid the aiming motion of the world
Aimless they mourned inert. The sluggish air
Oozed sullenly around their shapes, which lay
In attitudes as moveless and despaired
As those grey monoliths by heavenly ire
Uprooted from their bed of earth and spread
In crazy ranks involved like slaughtered things
Over the plain of Sennaar, when the pride
Of Babel sought to crown them with a pile
Of plinth that should outbreast the headlong clouds
And build its watchtower in the farthest star,
Dreadless to spy the Omnipotent; until
Scorned majesty cast the aspiring minds
Down in confusion, scattering the teeming throng,

And the divided tongues bred will to war.
So like the base of Babel in display
The Christian remnant in disastrous fall
Lay deadly. There lay Mary Magdalen
Mingling her tangled tresses in the dust
With jutted chin and wide and arid eyes,
Angered with horror, and her limbs outstreamed
In long and sinuous flow from her tense throat
Loose to her idle feet; while from set lips
Shadowed against the wall came one faint sob
Trembling into long silence, then one more,
Dividing time's slow breathings. Lazarus,
Her brother, sat at hand with rigid frown
Austere, and downward eyes, and heart on her.
And next was Simon with reflection shrunk,
His brow sunk on his arm-pent knees, and hands
Hooked vainly on the air, remembering
The long-relinquished sword; from the immense
And shaggy forest of his hair and beard
Protruded half his dry and yellow cheek
Creviced by wrinkles trickling from the eyes
Now clenched in desperate thought, as if his dreams
Were legions that bestrode the true and false
And, by tense will created, were to sweep
From the mind's marches. Only Thomas stirred
With working fingers and far-wandering eyes
And muttered discontent. But, for his foil,
Mary the Virgin, straight and slender-knit,
Sat with her hands upon her lap composed;
On her cold cheek lay winter unreproved,
And from her eyes still feeling, conscious pain

At ease within the hospitable haven
Of the accomplice heart, looked quiet out
Nor wrung one shudder from the graven lips;
But sorrow greeted had infused a calm
More royal than the fabulous repose
Distilled from changeless mirth in those bright dreams
That were the golden gods; so waited she,
Passive and unappalled, on twilight grey
And the fell mystery of approaching time.

Then in the silence, to their listening minds
Vocal with fearful tidings, Simon upraised
His forehead leonine and roaring voice,
Now shrilled and all unsinewed with amaze,
And, as to earless phantoms impotent
To learn his pity for their faded life,
Uttered his idle grief on the dead air:
"O mournful memories of a glorious birth!
You who with Christ warred on the world superb
To rid it of iniquity but fall
Before prevailing evil! Better despair
And know the worst, than cling to hope with fear
Of miseries unknown that may inflict
The malice unpredictable of foes!
Now all is lost, and with the envisaged truth
Fear perishes; our lord beyond reprieve
Is slain by potent will and soon in deed.
But harrowing this counsel that recalls
Frustration of the most heroic war
Waged ever on the earth, when our small league
Unarmed victorious battle joined with hosts

And in defeat upraised them. Memories
Of him, by whose strange prowess we prevailed
And by our own fidelity to him,
Embitter more bereavement. Bitter now
The image of the days when he required
Us from the kindly tedium of toil,
Combing our meager riches from the deep,
With summons all but wordless, while revealed
That silence ringing over Victory's horn
A world beyond the smallness of our world,
Dwarfing its skies; or when the bee-like stars,
Rifling the twilight of its honied trove,
Fluttered abroad out of the dying west
And smote the hills with adamantine beams,
We walked the uplands bleak from eve to morn
And steeped our tresses in the icy dews,
Forgetful of the time and weariness
For feeding on his words. Bitter the thought
Of how he won submission at a word
From multitudes and from his enemies
The flattery of fear. But bitterest
The memory of himself who now is doomed,
The paragon of men, fitted to lead
A soldier from his strife of blood to brave
More arduous conflict and debating ends
More terrible. Thomas, you recollect
How we discussed his words about himself?
Who can he be but—Is this blasphemy?
And yet I think it though I say it not,
And yet my thought confounds with what I see.
Our God in chains! Chains? They would flee his wrists,

And rip the lightning from the belching clouds
And whelm his foemen in their molten flood.
Yet when I think how all obeyed him, winds,
And waves, and sickness, even imperial death,
Devils and men, and other men more damned
Than devils, stooping to his naked word,
Then must I further think no conqueror
More worthy to be king of kings, more firm
And quiet, mightier, more undismayed,
With strength more plain in ease of exercise,
Has ever lorded men. I have been taught
While I held sword for this tormented land
That where is courage and the will to power
There forthwith is the power; each hundred years
Descends on men the fatal conqueror
With triple-kindled heart and purpose fixed
To weld the long-dissolving elements
Of man's society once more in one
Under his sway, nor lives there in the world
Who can repel his march. More Christ the Lord
Is proven in his acts; yet he is chained,
Chained by his natural slaves. O, I am dazed,
And the first tears that ever sought these eyes
Visit importunate. Why must our minds,
Too bleared to pierce beyond the here and now,
Be still constrained to trace the labyrinth
Of superhuman riddles to its heart
Or perish in confusion? We are mocked!"

He laughed with self-disdain. But Thomas cried:
"Simon, we mock ourselves, who are the dupes

Of our own creatures, hope and its awards
Fantastic. Lovers ever are bewitched,
And in their heroes the supreme deserts
And certain acquisition, that themselves
Confer, believe by natural gift to dwell,
Till in revulsion from the real they herd
With dreams and make their truth after their minds.
So by desire creative infinite
We crown our master king, discern in him
God's messenger expected, God himself,
And make anew our maker. He has gone
Before us with extravagance of faith
In truth infallible of promises
Conjured from his aspiring will, until
The solid truth that lives outside the mind,
Spurning its nebulous pretender, now
Has scattered us and chained him. Yet remark
How at the first he shrank from sovereignty,
Would not be titled Christ, nor yet the Good,
Till, of his power and royal mold of mind
By homage universal made expert,
He with this sway inclined to ease the throes
Of suffering men. Then this divine desire,
That men call pity, touched such vehemence
That, in his thought resembling destiny
Inevitable, it interpreted
As might invincible his spirit's power,
Great among men but single and confined;
And this inexorable pity seemed
To manifest command from the Divine,
Writ in his nature, to redeem the world.

What works he wrought! But were they yet divine?
Around the altars of the ethnic gods,
Infernal Jove and his familiars,
Such deeds are rumored, such dim prophecies
As net small truths in wide uncertainties
And aimed conjectures. He has healed the sick?
But who will not confess to health when told
Of cure by the wise leech? He raised the dead?
Which of us saw the breath-unmisted glass?
Stilled he the tempest or foresaw the calm?
Walked he the waves or but the foamy marge
Telling our salt-locked eyes through spumy whorls
What they would though it were not? The reply
Presses my ears: Demented heroism!
Noble delusion! Yet some keep in me
Is formidable to my denying mind.
How can the heart be true when reason lies?
Or is it reason that corrects the heart?
Perhaps the ruin of the thing I love
Has wrought such hatred of all life that I
To hatred even of what I love descend,
Despising it for its inconstancy;
Yet but dissimulated perfidy
It is to make occasion of distress
To impute infidelity. This strife
Is grievous between contrary desires,
When either victory crowns me forlorn
Of what is loved and vanquished. So to end
And choose the nobler faction, though with loss
Of prudence and my own indemnity:
Whoever he may be, I am all his,

And rather with our master choose to die
Than live of him deprived. Now mine to seek,
To save or die, and to forsake this strife
With ignorance."
                    The rest heard, frowning some,
Not moved in faith nor wroth with unbelief
But with words comfortless, while the voice waned
In mused murmurs like an ebbing tide
Indrawn to the lonely bosom of the main;
So with soft self-communing he lost heed
Of all their avid ears, and at the last
Leaped up to seek the morning. But the door
Just widened as he moved and, thresholded,
A meager boy with ruddy locks unkempt,
In tattered and ungirdled tunic clad,
Stood dallying moody, then with sudden shriek
And outspread hands to Mary Virgin fled
And plunged his sobbing face upon her lap;
A space he sobbed while understanding all
Regarded him, then cried with head flung back:
"Mother of Jesus, they have taken him,
Taken him, taken him, and roped his arms
Fast as that truant slave's that yesterday
The soldiers caught without. I saw him, I,
Towering amongst his foemen, dazzling white
And terrible as a heron tarred by daws.
O, the brave port of him! He ruled with glance
More mighty from his bonds than Pilate rules
From the imperial seat when he presides
Over the Roman games; I followed close
To note how all eyes cowered but his own

And mold me to his hardihood, till one
Stripped me and I must hasten back to home
To get my brother's tunic. Is he killed?
Tell me, what news? We were such friends, such friends,
That when he is away the other lads
To me are hateful, and at home I find
Thought of tomorrow empty, and the fields,
Where he told stories and described to us
His country, are in gloom. But though I cry,
Mother, I can be bold; for I have safe
Three arrows for my bow, for Caiaphas
One, and for Annas one, for Judas one;
They are well-notched, well-feathered, and well-barbed;
Can I but creep up close I can despatch
One through each traitor heart and still its beat;
Then Christ is free. Is it not rightly done
Like the great Trojan heroes to intend
To slay my friend's betrayers? What think you?"
But Mary said "Poor child, too young for grief,
You love unwitting that to help my son
Is to wound none, to love him not to hate;
Not so shall he prevail, but in your life
When in your patience his shall live again.
Be not abroad today but keep within,
And go to Magdalen and comfort her
By suffering her comfort!"
                      But forthwith
The voice of Magdalen in level tones
Broke out deep-throated like the murmur far
Of thralls complaining in a hollow mine:
"Call me not Magdalen; she died with Christ

Betrayed to die, and the abandoned past
Resumes to dwell with lamentable shades.
But if there be companionship in grief
Or bitterness can sweeten bitterness,
Then, stricken child, possess with my last love
What solace you can glean by pondering
A misery that is not matched by yours.
I am the relic of that Magdalen
Who once stunned with the rapture of their eyes
The men who looked on me, and walked the earth
To shame its riches like a visitant
From burnished fields in the immortal sun,
Which in my eyes and hair and ardent breath
And all the lightnings of my tenderness
Was famed still to inhabit with delight.
O boy not yet too old to feel the pang
That urges woman, lords of all things seen,
Men soon forget their human indigence
And irresistible conceive their power;
But I, the flower of all womanhood,
Knew that my virtue from my first of life
Must by devotion to another's cause
And in the glory of his victory
Fulfil its utmost worth. Only if knit
To some aspiring spirit and supreme
By love accepted by his love returned,
Could I his valor, strength, accomplishment
Seize for my own, who by the sale of self
Should change me for a hero. For to love
Is to retreat from self and to invest
The thoughts of the beloved by regard

Intuitive, if granted is desire,
And to ignore all selfish pain and bliss
For eagerness to gaze on joy achieved
By the adopted self (for I in love
Am learned). Now seek not to understand
Too much of this, for knowledge is for age
And can untimely purchased overwhelm
The feeble innocence. I, rebel made
By need insistent, in the secret night
Sought for my lover among many men
In vain. For they desired but what they saw,
This bodily husk, and for their own behoof;
I at the selfsame gate defeated paused
Nor won to insight. Ever two walls of flesh
Divided soul from soul and sight from sight;
Ever the captive essence in the brain
Pleaded through embassy of words or hands,
Tokens inept, across disastrous space
Where knowledge perished. In my lover's hall
At dusk between the pillars we would sit
To hear the passionate bird distil her grief
Over the glassy pool, and from the stars,
Those candid counselors of steadfastness,
To drink new fervor for the quest of love,—
Yet but to stay that quest; for I, absorbed
In contemplation of the night's fair face
Impressed upon my sense, my weariness
Of seeking and my baffled efforts knew
In my distraction, and that deep in each
The solitary mind contained its world
Impervious save to its shadowy brood.

So after many foilings I, revulsed,
To thwart the law devised to thwart my end
By law devised, turned to revolt professed,
And hopeless, yet for rancor, plied my art
About the crossways, where my irised robes
And flowered hair enticed the strolling world
To gird at nature, to avenge their irk
On its artificer, by fortunate sin
To give the lie to conscience. Thus was fallen
The famous Magdalen, and the norm superb
Of beauty's title in the various world
Devoted was by chosen servitude
To be the fodder of barbarian lust.
But time came when, intolerant with scorn,
The folk would stone me for my heart of stone,
And, as confounding as the sun in storm
Tedding the skirts of turmoil, came the Lord
And ripped me from the volley. They withdrew
And left me thankless for my weary life
Crouched at his feet. But, as resentful I
Looked up and pondered his confronting eyes
(There where the veil of mind is scantiest),
I saw there of my beauty no regard
But in his thought the likeness of my soul,
And it was foul and loved. Then I discerned
That he besought no recompense of me,
But loved me only for my good, aware
Of all my evil. So none hitherto
Had ever truly loved me as this man,
Except my parents dead, whose love of all
On earth is likest God's; and in the mind

That contemplated mine immediately
I knew that God inhabited. He asked
Had any man condemned me; I replied
Unto him 'No man, Lord' and with the words
'Neither do I condemn you; now arise
And sin no more!' he turned aside and passed
Into a narrow street beyond my sight.
Then bent my fearless and defiant soul
To unaccustomed tears, with passions rent
Of grief and gladness. Heavenly decree
Inscribed upon my need had given me
To a divine alliance, not in flesh
Nor to be consummated on the earth,
But by immortal vision mutual
Hereafter as God wills. But penitence,
Such as they only know who their own hearts'
Most high necessities betray, immersed
Therewith my consciousness, who had traduced
The oracle in my nativity
By mutiny to nature and to Christ
Unfaithful impulse. O abandoned soul,
Yet hopeless not, since superhuman love
Alone still unestranged left me despoiled
Of all but its endowment infinite.
So, spurred by terror lest my undesert
Should move my master to revoke his gift,
I, to endorse it by my heart declared
Fixed in eternal sorrow and new love,
Enquired for him and in the leper's house
Fled headlong to his feet. There I, constrained
To give myself not only in desire,

Found me a delegate. As from of old
The priests of the Most High have sacrificed
Young lambs and the rich firstlings of the boughs
In witness of the rights of God on man,
I shed the soul of the alabaster shards
Upon the forehead of my lord divine,
And won my conqueror and destiny.
For if the honeyed shrubs of India
And all the silken corbeils of the waves
That line with fragrant ambergris the south,
If all the lost breaths of Semiramis,
Upgathered in one rose, and in its mate
The odors that her eyes wooed from the blooms
Of her winged gardens, if all incense sweet,
That ever since the making of the world
Loaded the vernal winds and warbling boughs,
Had been distilled in that faint flow of nard,
Love still had steeped it with prevailing fume
And scented fragrance with its absolute.
Thus was the bond so coveted confirmed
That now frustrated is with such defeat
Irreparable of the one desire
That to the very porches of despair
Each moment summons me. O God, to take
The way abrupt into forgetfulness
Explored by the impatient of defeat,
Or that fidelity closed not the breach
To refuge! But my death it is to live."

She paused entranced and introspect; but they
Paled and a silence chill came down on them,

For each saw imaged in her woe his own.
And suddenly the door sprang wide and stood
Peter within, tense as a fugitive,
With harassed eyes whence gushed reluctant tears,
And groaned and cried to them: "O you forlorn,
Yet better thus forlorn, sundered by fear
And natural weakness from heroic Christ
Of whom unworthy nature renders us,
Than by elected treason and the act
Supreme of self autonomous to defame
His native dignity. Unholy choice,
And terrible the memory thereof,
For I, of this small province prince, am he
That has forsworn its faith and Jesus Christ.
O that the past, even as the future is,
Were to will docile, nor inexorably
Loaded the soul with consequential dues,
Or to have died an hour since, nor defined
Forever true that Peter scorned his lord!
O miserable and for vengeance ripe
Who late was honored in the noblest band
That ever ventured in the cause of truth!
I followed him with John to the false court
Where they condemned him, but while I delayed
They probed me if I knew him and (for shame
Or fear no matter; the deed curses me)
I told them over he was not my lord.
Then he, with all their railings on his head,
Came out, needing his only friend, and me
Saw but no friend; and in those eyes I read
No dispensation from the law of things

Nor pardon but by self-destruction shown,
Yet what destruction will implore return
Of honor forfeited I read therein:
Not the self-vengeance of the Roman code,
To take from off the earth a thing defiled,
The bane of its own purpose, and curtail
The debt by sealing source of further wrong,
But self-annihilation by self-change,
By putting on the new to slay the old,
To straighten out the crooked in desire,
Deny denial by the faithful deed,
And with the contrite heart to crush the crime.
Hence these hot tears of wrath against myself
As truly as of sorrow, and the pledge
Of a heart tempered in my falsehood's fires
Curveless and keen to battle to what end
Despotic time and time's great despot, God,
Have me assigned. Hence this entreaty strong,
O men of Christ, his likeness to resume,
Your faith and purpose to obey his will,
Though dark now his behests. O in those eyes
I saw the truth forever: he is God;
There no dismay, but confident command,
Deliberate ordering of circumstance
To his self-meditated end, though strange
To our small wits the means; and in those eyes
The old solicitude and kingship throned,
Proclaiming him with undiminished fire,
As once on Tabor in his whole aspect,
The goodly term whose name unrecognized
In the dissatisfaction of the will

Resides when it achieves its hopes on earth.
Him must we seek, though now his path be dark
And all the highways of the world be bright;
And seeking is unquestioning to wait."
He strove with tears and with his whelming grief
That from his dominant mind they might take strength.
But Mary Virgin cried: "Peter, we all
Know grief, repentance, sore perplexity,
But one is here whose mind is like a lamp
Lit by its converse with the blessed dead,
The wise ones in the vestibule of joy
Called Limbo, where they tarried to await
Their call to God, and he his call again
To this dim world and cold. O Lazarus,
Of you we all expect deliverance
From this oppressive mystery, and light
Corrupting ignorance, which binds the soul
And all its ends frustrates. I too entreat,
For I am groping too in devious glooms,
And know but that my son is good, his deeds
Divine and right, even his embrace of pain,
Though his intent be hid."
                            And Lazarus
Took hesitating speech. "O Mary Queen,
The presage of irreparable ruin
To all that is beloved conjures grief
So mortal that the mind halts from its quest,
Blind but to its own pain. Yet to contend
Against despair though hopeless and in faith
Through darkness to endure foremost deserve
Renown immortal. Such renown is ours

Already, who have trusted in the Lord,
Though adverse machinations have contrived
To utter his destruction. But not this
Our chief reward, for sorrow is a pledge
And the interpretation of our pain
Omen of triumph. Ever what is made,
Though fair, is from the acme increate
Deficient, so laboriously must seek
Its fulness in the illimitable main
Whence first it borrowed being. But this world,
Fashioned in time by the Eternal, moves
Nor to perfection nor more near can grow
In form to the Allperfect but by change
Destroying to reform; so by process
Of births and deaths of earth's particulars
The Godlike slow is formed. This universe
Of things articulated to one world
In infinite unbeing pendulous
Quits itself rather than refrain from him
To whom it blind sweeps upward in desire;
Whose parts in search of good through others force
Obliterating path, but, marred with toil,
Brandish their own destruction and in ruin
Take victory. Yet final victory
Must be to the immortal, and on earth
None is immortal but the spirit of man,
Alone which can pursue on God nor wane
In the achievement, for unchanged it dons
Divinity by knowledge. To exalt
The progress of the spirit all things else
Even in the outer firmament conspire

As to their proper triumph, but of all
Most man himself. For he by fragile flesh
Submerged in the corrosive flux of time
Chains the royal spirit in the bewildering fray
Whence to be free it yearns. That liberty
From man's prolonged corruption and the stress
Of the evolving world is wrought; all things
Must perish to promote the spirit's quest,
Even the hospitable body, while
Itself its vision seeks and at that goal
The universe is crowned. Yet it is crowned
By pain, for change is the relinquishing
Of being and of self and this is pain;
Man's part at last prevails embracing God,
But by man's dust that wastes itself to feed
The spirit's glory at the term of toil.
So in our travail is the world reborn,
And the procession of the dolorous years
Brings forth and whelms new creatures, which meanwhile
By suffering move to grasp the infinite
And conquer in our minds, when through their pain
These persevere to God and evermore
Become the trophies of creation's war.
But to this happy end not all arrive
Of men, for what is lovable on earth
Must perish soon or late, and who by love
Deliberate identify their fate
With what must pass, from the Ideal turn
Which by accepted loss of all desire
On earth and instant anguish is attained.
We are too weak to conquer any power

But the Omnipotent, to gain a hope
That is not infinite, with constancy
To love what is not all; and our frail hands
Must drop their coveted burdens, seek we not
Fulfilment of ambition infinite,
To which the way is change, relentless grief.
So you, who in the plenitude of loss,
Though staggering, still steadfast cling to God,
Chosen declare your destiny with those
Who shall achieve the world, and worthily
Pursue with Christ his bliss. But that pursuit
Is waged beside its term; for Christ excels
All patience, who, unstaggering in will,
More than what death can bring to us endures
Yet moves not to repulse. Such constancy
Is proper but to God who by his act
Alone eternal is, unchangeable;
So Christ is God, and we in ignorance
Have stood with him next to our destiny."

Then Simon cried: "But why should God desert
His everlasting quiet to endue
Our sorrow and the servile vest of pain?"
And Lazarus resumed: "Something of this
I can show, but uncertainly. When first
Man defied God, and the victorious flight
Of being to its source was curved awry
By the secession of the vanward head,
Then all the generations of our race
That should in time ensue inherited
The warped mind of the parent, ignorance

Ingrafted and degenerate desire,
Declension from the way to God. Nor earth
Could bear a saviour, for the lord of things
Had wandered and the impotent to rule
Must follow hard to universal fall;
Irreparable fall, unless, remorsed,
Man's maker should remake his broken man
And rein the second chaos till it soared
Again on Godward wing. Yet only man
Could rescue man, for since the will had swerved
By free intrinsic power, nor violence
Nor necessary moment but alone
Self-chosen repudiation could redress
Its self-decreed rebellion. So if time
Bears its redeemer to the ruined world
He shall in unity be God and man,
Who by first taking in his flesh the change
Must first bear torment. Such these years have borne,
And on this present pinnacle of time
The curse that blasted Eden's fadeless leaves
And brought the meed of death to all our pain
Is revocable made and God resumes
His work by taking human agony.
Jesus, the son of God and Mary maid,
Comes with the sorrows of the race of man
Crushing his dedicated head, more grave
Than on the mythic giant hung the weight
Of heaven and earth while he with tensed breast
Shouldered the skies and braced his struggling soles
Against the stubborn basement of the glebe.

95

Today Christ consummates but with such wealth
Of agony in death as will surpass
The function of redemption, and this pain
Is also purposed; for ourselves alone
Can break our flight to God who in free will
Have power to revolt or to be loyal;
So to entice our choice he undertakes
This passion with extravagance of woe
To manifest extravagance of love,
And to reveal the guidance of the world
Renewed and indefectible, for God
Has entered his creation. And today
We suffer in his pain, for in that pain
Is wrought our change and the strayed world revoked
Back towards its heavenly repose. But he,
In all the tribulations that the years
On us inflict, will suffer in our pain,
While we like other Christs fulfil his work
By molding to the fashion of his mind
The form of human effort. Unreprieved
The passion in this city now begun
Will last until the end of time and change
Revived in anguished man vicariously
Who suffers for the need of God. So we,
Smit with immeasurable loss, discern
In pain the process of reversion slow
To the high zone of spiritual birth,
Where from eternal Being sprang our souls;
With such transfiguration medicining
The weariness of grief, to persevere

Let us be fortified; for now our task
Is to endure, to strive, to hold the truth,
To take the lot of Christ."
                              So Lazarus.
But they with bended heads and eyes withdrawn
Upon the knowledge of divine desire
Sat rapt, and, as the light grew resolute
And morning stood established in the air,
The tumult of their minds and of their hearts
Subsided with the gradual surprise
Of joy that knowledge to the upright brings;
And to their wills unpurposed and relaxed
Came new determination to advance
The immortal cause and valor to endure,
Till peace pervaded them, and Thomas even
Sat wordless and inert, and Magdalen
Stared eager with the awe of hope returned.
Then suddenly one clamored from the door,
John, who unseen had entered and lent ear:
"Arise, and take the truth that we have known
But feared to eye for its immensity:
The Everlasting shapes him to our sight,
Clothes him in human, takes and gives man's love,
Now writhes in pain corporeal. I knew
Godhead in him when in the council hall
I saw him doomed and striped, while, plunged by love
In the one grief and agony with him,
My mind swooned listless as a mirroring pool
That weeps but acts not for the things it sees;
The deed I should have wrought formed it too late
In my conceit, or idly I mused hope

Of heavenly intervention lest its doubt
Should show the need to act, while every pulse
Of time enthralled him more to hungry death
And damned me for unmettled and a slave
To sterile fantasy. Enough! Needs now
To bear my own unworth and to undo
By further courage. What love prompts is wise,
And I must join him now if beyond time
I bide with him forever; this my choice,
To seek him and to flout the priests or lone
Or with whatever comrades will of you."

Then said the Virgin Mother: "Think not, John,
So meanly of me as to deem that I,
His mother, can forbear his last regard
Nor with my tears sprinkled upon his breast
Embalm whom other spices are denied."
And Magdalen cried: "And I go with you,
Who know one only good, to be with him,
And in his loss the least of evils, death,
And first of favors to be quenched with him."
Hard on her words swift from the city's heart
There crashed the tumult of a thousand throats
In vengeful uproar raised: "Crucify him!"
And they arose, unlatched the door, and straight
With proud, untroubled eyes and mien resolved
Silent they passed into the hostile day.

HERE ON the patient tables of my mind
Scored by the style that works their vacancy
With figured knowledge, or by subtler touch
Or natural instruction of the sense
Induced, in other places and new hands
The tale divine unfolds. Therein I read
How, while those parleyed from despair and woe
To earnest joy, from the stone chamber dark,
Where by remorseless prescience divine
The dark was painted with the mocking forms
Of future pangs, some haled the Son of God
To meet the dread foreseen. As on the street
He issued with his guards, the priests afar
Tarried at gaze on dazzling milken mules,
By Annas reined to draw the loitering crowds
While at his shoulder Caiaphas intent
Played the obsequious deacon. At the sight
Of the fierce autocrat and the calm Christ
Confronted inimical, tremulous

99

The idlers scattered in the early ways
Cried and ran up in haste to savor sharp
The promised spectacle, as of two hosts
Instructed for exterminative war;
And who saw Jesus from afar despised
For broken and defeated gait, but those
Who saw his face at hand marveled in mind
At look of one who acted and achieved
Triumphant, nor endured alone, his smart;
Yet but the noblest felt a fearful joy,
Not as at evil fettered, but because
His fallen power pointed their smallness less.
And as the train moved in funereal pace
Each renewed cry echoed in distant cry,
Until the confines of the city's walls
Sounded with tumult multiplied, and swelled
To restless uproar near, while from each street
Men who were not their being nor endured
By what they were came hosting to defy
Him who had called them from the naked void.

So, both with equal purpose to achieve
By the same instrument opposing ends,
Annas and Jesus in succession staid
And solemn retinue advanced, while surged
With eager question or in reverence hushed
The populace expectant on their rear.
But as they went Annas to Caiaphas
Spoke low and tense: "Caiaphas, this first step
Forces all future, rowels the shrinking will
Like an indwelling devil that will let

Rest to our feet till we be crowned or lost,
Generates perils fecund of their kind
That slay or bridge to triumph; but it bends
To act and leaves our self-direction sound
And choice of issue; here security
Lies if we act by forethought, nor permit
Occasion to surprise us, nor the care
Of evil consequence to lame attack.
What if the issue of victorious feat
Be evil? Is not power its issue too,
Power, the medicine of all mortal ills?
So shall our deed beget the remedy
Twin with the bane, and phantoms are our dread
Who fear the progeny of any act
Conducted to the conquest of our end.
No more of that, lest talk of fear raise fear
And make us parasites of our desire
Who are its natural masters! For myself
The mere constraint to act I gladly bear
Keeping the reins of exit. Let us, now
That we attain the field where first we strive,
Slip these raw witnesses that shook of late
Our prosperous passage, and before the folk
Spring to the question straight; the Nazarene
Is firmer than to gainsay the said word.
But first I must acquaint them with distrust
Of him whom they must damn."

> The train drew nigh

Where loomed a mighty theater of thrones
Of somber porphyry hewn at the coign
Of the tremendous fane, whose horrent thighs

Marmoreal or greaved with burnished gold,
Clothed in the lawn of morning, passionate
And terrible retorts of fire flung down
Upon the curial tiers. Here was the place
Where the high pontiffs met in court supreme
To bare their judgments just. First Caiaphas
Climbed to the judgment seat, and to the cirque
The priests in silence menacing advanced,
Sat, and maintained deliberative hush
While Jesus was brought in and stood lax-limbed
And bruised and heavy-headed, and the mob
Surged to his view. Then all in silence stood,
Intending breathless, while spoke Annas these:
"Hebrews, elected children of high God!
For though inheritors of ravished fields,
Ravished unjustly, still irrevocably
Stands the Allhighest's gift. Fidelity
To him enjoins fidelity to defend
His trust this ancient city and the lands
Won by the valor of our fathers dead,
Twice hallowed then, by heavenly command
As well as memory and the toil obscure
That all our generations have bestowed
To raise these fruitful pastures. Though our hands
Be tied still the unconquered spirit free
Waits girt to counsel the redemptive sword
When time shall offer it; meanwhile all hope
Lies in the aid of God and union fast
With us, your lovers and God-chosen guides,
With what of former glory still invests
The shards of Juda's power; for on that base

God will rebuild the temple of our pride
By Gentiles overthrown. O, in this strait
If one should wrest the buttress of our hope,
The last sole implement of liberty,
Which is the health of states, what death for him
Should be too sudden, what excessive pain,
What scorn undue upon his memory?
Lo, here he stands, one festering in the shame
Of perfidy unveiled, who schemes the rent
Of Israel, the weaning of your loves
From the high Sanhedrin, the unitive form
Of the spread commonwealth and tie unique
Against immersion and the loss of self
In the devouring Roman! He has bragged
To be divine, and in one effort striven
To draw your hearts from us and Israel
To Israel's latest idol and false god,
Himself, and alienated God the true
From aiding the blasphemers, him and those
Whom he has cozened to his following
By simulated tenderness and saws
Of hollow wisdom. For a little sway
He, an ignobler Samson, would uproot
The pillars of our sieged liberty
And whelm us in the Roman with himself.
To him then who would mulct us of all aid
Divine or human, and a ravaged prey
Present us to our captors, what the doom
In justice to requite? I can descry
God and the saints of eld, who whirled God's sword
Against the proud and fornicating powers

Who once insulted in this land, expect
Response of sacred anger. I could weep
If Juda's ruin must by Juda grow,
If what the oppressor maimed treason must slay
And we fail God and fail, we waterveined,
Ourselves by soft surrender of our rights,
Our homes, and lovely fields, and cities haught,
To spare a rebel's mischief. Be it not so,
O constant people! But, before we judge,
Hear first one witness, hear his lips proclaim
His own damnation! Caiaphas, question him!"

Then Caiaphas stood in the judgment seat
From the dim summit louring like a cloud
That silent stealing over the drowsy north
Hangs meditating havoc; then he loosed
The mournful thunder of his voice which rolled
From airy distance round the ears of Christ:
"I charge you by the living God to say
Are you the Son of God?" Jesus forthwith
Upraised his sunken brow and solemn-toned
Made answer: "I but say what you have heard
This night before: I am the Son of God
Indeed, destined to judge all times and tribes
When come God's angels to dissolve the world."
Straight Annas cried "You hear his wickedness,
From his own lips you hear. Name you his death
That soon we may despatch!" A fearful hush
Ensued; for those who loved a moment stood
Wrought by amazement at Christ's protest plain
Into ambiguous counsel, but the rest

Swung by the tide of Annas' conquering words
Nor fixed by noble judgment, nor the weak
Uncomforted to see the fall of power
In one but late their peer, expected but
A leader for their voice. Then came a shout
With sudden hatred hoarse "Crucify him!"
And, like a flood that bursts in one swift roar
Its sluice distent, from the wide multitude
A shriek that echoed in the heights of towers
And shattered the tranquillity of hearts
Broke forth imperative "Crucify him!"
And sprang the foremost with blind fury forth
With outstretched hands to seize, but vigilant
Gathered the guards into their center Christ
And stood in phalanx while the great throng reeled
Backward in disarray and wary hung
In dubious threat of pillage. Annas cried
Forthwith "Hold, you avengers heady, lead
The traitor to the threshold of the keep,
That we may sue the Roman for his death
Nor stir for ours the eagle's jealousy!
We shall prevent you there." The serried knot
Of guards broke through the objurgating mob,
And bearing Christ sought the Antonian towers,
While joyous with the deathlust swirled the crowd
Behind their measured march. Annas delayed
One moment and to Caiaphas exclaimed:
"Now, past the bridle of our will to check,
The deed is running; when no counsels firm
Direct the choice then the first passion grows
In reason's place to motive and outcries

Thought in the mind's ear, till calamity
Trammels the issue and snuffs rage with fear.
The witless people, pregnant now with spleen,
Since blood insurgent has their reason stunned,
Will push it to the last, if happy fruit
Attends their effort; let us now pursue
And from the Roman pluck the happy fruit!"

But as he turned one caught his cloak, and there
Clung Judas, wildeyed with entreaty tense,
Who cried "Stay, Annas, shed not guiltless blood!
For guiltless blood conjures chastisers dire
Out of the secret deep where lurk the powers
That champion the wronged dead; take back your coin,
Nor jeopard me to spill the blood of Christ
That puts in fee our own!" But Annas said:
"Your deed is sold, is ours to use at will,
And you must bide what we shall breed of it,
Too late abhorred. Your conscience is your own,
And yours the money; what your craven soul
Of phantom wound converts to sensible
Keep, and your pay to medicine it!" So he
And with cool scorn strode after Caiaphas.
But Judas stood alone with his despair
Full in the place of judgment, with the coins,
The witness of his crime, clenched in his palm,
And suddenly beheld the vast encinct
Of empty thrones in grey and vengeful height
Beetling upon him; peopling the stones
With souls from his bewildered fancy, shrieked
Then with contempt he laughed and flung the coins

With dismal ring upon the pavement down
And headlong fled. Nor may the Muse delay,
Though heavenly, to spy what God must spy,
To follow him to horror, though obscure
How horror such can ride the wave of song,
Sweet song, wave of the well of quietness.

Beyond the gates he fled, out of the day
And the bright haunts of life to a lone vale,
A mangled place where shattered trunks of stone,
Hurled by the first pulse of the infant Time,
In towers reared and monstrous parapets
Nodding unwrought destruction; columns erect
Leaned trembling, in the stagnant dim of air
Held ever hovering, and with shadow cast
Singled their prey, when Time should single them
To fall to ravage; and gigantic flags
Of stone compiled in companies uncouth
Lay prostrate, gross and unconsidering
As if in slumber slain. Hither no beast
To mumble the degged scraw, no wild birds strayed,
No life heaved but the predatory worm
And one distorted trunk that slaked its boughs
Upon the meager ooze of the rank mold.
Here where death mated with perpetual
Menace of deadlier resurrection
Came Judas with his noose, and, questioning
His state for counsel or expedient,
To counterfeit pity in solitude
Speaking aloud, he fed on his own words:

"Too late abhorred," he said. "So here my road
Is ended, and my life's economy
Gains but the darkness. O disastrous fate!
Quenched is achievement, hope, nature itself
Distorted by irrevocable revolt
And abdication of my heritage.
Torment intolerable is this self
Thus thwarted and alive to contemplate;
Evil I suffer not, evil I am,
Nor ever can consort with good again
Till I dissolve. Why must I know that all
That I desired was in the Nazarene
Alone incarnate, only when forsworn
Now beyond call? What has frustrated me?
Not my own choice, for lives there one whose will
Repudiates ambition recognized
And to his hand? Nor this my guilt invokes,
For nature, which has fashioned me in need,
My master and immutable desire
Has bound to seek my sustenance; and Christ,
Though arbiter of immeasurable wealth,
Hid his resources and all subsidy
To my necessity denied. What way
Remained to staunch the soul's anxiety
Save to negotiate the lean reward
Offered for his betrayal? So I moved
His capture and unwittingly condemned
My soul to the surrender of its good.
Yet who can chide me for obedience
To the commands of nature that enforce
Inexorably their ends? Not mine the blame;

But who will Christ absolve? Him who possessed
The secret treasures of the teeming world
By stewardship divine, my craving knew,
Yet to compel my slavery to him
Not a mite tendered? Nay, enough had been
To slake my longing and to anchor fast
My whole devotion to reveal to me
Unique his might and indefeasible
His partisans to furnish against want;
Yet, when he could, revealed he nought but grace
Airy and unsubstantial to be won
In the chill dwelling of the joyless dead.
Surely he wrought my fall, purposed perhaps,
Who wantonly and with foreknowledge full
Permitted my intents their headlong course!
And is not Annas guilty? He the first
Making me victim of his own designs,
Enticed me to my ruin, pitied not
My peril nor relented, when, aware
Of all my error, I entreated him,
And to my fall abandoned me. The rest,
My fellows in the twelve, incurious
Of my distress, with smothered enmity
And passive hands saw me in ignorance
Slide to misfortune. Nay, but God himself
Who made my nature, made my nature's sin
Its necessary progeny, and willed
Forever my rebellion unto him.
O wisdom late, appeasing with despair
And knowledge that misfortune comes no more
Since all is lost! I never had a friend

Nor knew the charity of which Christ speaks
To be but in his words; and now all those
Who know me, all the enemies of Christ,
His followers, himself, and God supreme
Have duped me and rejected, driven forth
Lonely to this damnation. O you fiends!
No other hell can be beyond this world,
Where men by others pitilessly spurned,
Each in his incommunicable thought
Immured and all forgotten, burn and groan
In their intrinsic fires. Yet would that God
And men and the wide universe of things
Had me forgotten, nor unanimous
Conspired to glut their cruelty on me,
Their playball, and to laceration long
And gradual, but utter, me consigned
For triumph, theirs; though ere the world began
God had designed my nature to destroy!
Am I then desolation's monument
To universal hatred predefined,
Because to be that being I have dared
Which the eternal law of things detests,
Though dignified, and all unrighteously,
The man who to his own desires is true
Nor them forsakes to pleasure, like a slave,
Any authority? But season fails
And thought is over; now but hate abides,
Hate for the whole of things, my enemies,
And in this place defiance. Cursed be Christ,
Health to his killers, and to him such pangs
As he complacent saw descend on me

Ere the dogs rend him dead! Annas be cursed
And shrivel in his hand the fruit of scheme
And whisper to the Roman, unto whom
I here bequeath my vengeance! Cursed be all
Unmoved who watched my ruin, may they find
No saviour in their need! But, over all,
The ancient evil, you whom men adore,
I with my power execrate. You make
To err us, agents for the deeds you fear,
Or to wring reason from us to torment;
O who will pardon you? Forsake your ease
And hear the maledictions of your work
Immune made by extremity of ill!
Could I to introspection turn your mind
On its own horror, man should be redressed,
For yours is greater misery than all pain,
Pain to have made. This then I wish for you,
That you may know yourself abominable,
And for self-hatred perish by your act
With all your works; let sometime justice reach
And knowledge to the highest, who will call
Righteous extinction down on the ill world,
Burning like Sodom by the bitter lake,
And him its fell original, and give
To solitary space and sterile night
Eternal empire and impregnable
Where being once offended! Be accursed
The commonwealth and common wickedness
Of all that is! Now to the utmost bound
Of the world driven dares one man at last
Defend his faculties to nourish life

Against the congregated enmity
Of the immense of God and all his works.
Let God beware! For summoned from the void
(So say the legends that foretell the truth)
Gods have already risen to dethrone
A deity unworthy and effete.
Now at my summons shall not one arise
And armed with fiery globes, the thunderbolt
Surpassing, and the valor of the just
Trumpet at heaven's rampart? Come, revenge!
But whence, since all is God's and they who sought
Failed for their evil? Ah, accursed am I,
Constrained thus with my small and single strength
The universe of power to indict
And to oppose in enemy. O plague
But to exist and who begot my life
Here to revile! No more, I must evade
This horror that I am, while thought remains,
By ending me; oblivion may descend
And peace in that incalculable clime
In which the journey of the soul is lost
To living eyes. Death only can release
When being to itself is agony."
Then, on a boulder rising, to the bough
He drew the thong and to his neck the noose,
One moment paused, and spoke: "Now strives my soul
Against its passage; whither do I leap?
O God, those eyes again! They swell not now
With humid pity, but with wrathful threat,
And secret might seduces me to plunge

Beyond my will's strength to inhabit day
Into their obscure deep. Ah, save me, hell!
Pity me, demons, rebels, malices!
I fall into the angry eyes of God!
O hatred, where is power?" And Judas leaped.

Bⁿ UT PILATE on the height of the gaunt tower
Looked on the stolen realm of Israel
Under the morning, and divined the will
That kindling slowly in the incensed land
Menaced the Roman seizure. Far below
The sullen city, in the vapored dews
Floating, arose in ruddy terraces
Of mansions piled, wave upon wave, to sink
Prone on the crest of Sion. In the name
Of many a street and palace tall preserved
Unaging, vanished princesses lived on
Whose beauty had ensnared the giant strength
Of Sion's lords and broached the gates superb.
There in their middle solitary stood
A tower lifeless as with trance of grief
Remembering Mariamne, loved and slain,
Last scion of the Asmonean line,
That smote from Bethzur to the salty lake
Single the Gentile phalanx and laid low

115

The embattled might of Macedon. Beyond
An uncouth wilderness to Canaan stretched
Where jagged breasts of adamantine crag
Started above the sapphire mists and hung
Troubled as if in swoon; their flanks abrupt,
Brindled with the impenetrable glooms
That mantled the recesses of their chasms,
Headlong fell downward till the Jordan's flood,
Invisible and silent, darkly strode
Through the cleft heights to feed the inland sea,
In whose salt womb the anguish and despair
That whelmed the impious cities, when their lusts
Raked lightning from the arsenals of God,
Sleep till their second birth. And on the verge
Of furthest sight Tabor and Carmel raised
Half to the day-star's height their iron horns,
Whence drives the Kishon from the pastoral land
His limpid waters. There the munching kine
Dappled with purple shade stand at the cud,
In grass and pensive bugle-blooms that sweep
Their teeming udders, moody all the noon,
And still beneath the boughs at evening stand.
Around him bent in homage Pilate sensed
His wide domain, until he backward glanced
And saw with anger-clouded eyes, precinct
Unconquered yet, the temple insolent,
Barring with front imperative his gaze,
Abruptly with forbidding splendor state
The frontier of his sway. But as he frowned
One stood between the challenge and his wrath
And laid it calm. He to her:

"Claudia,
Untimely, sweet, with ever-wooing eyes
You make distraint of valor in the hour
When I must steel my heart. Perfidious love
That bids me hate the duty of grim war
And feast on you my vision and my mind
On your delightful words! No stranger spell
Wrought Cytherea and her silver doves
Over the god of arms than when your cheek
Lies on my harness thus and overwhelms
By yielding. Now you conquer and my care
Forgets its bitterness."
                              But she replied:
"Lord of my heart and fate under high God,
If conquered is your care then I demand
Possession by my right of conqueror.
Surrender to my knowledge your alarm
By telling me its cause, that I forthwith
May slay it with my forecast, and retrieve
My husband from all dread!"
                              Then he to her
Answered: "O daughter of the Claudian seed,
The power that works in us fashions in each
His purpose and his fate, though laboring
Long with our obduracy. So have I striven
Through many lands and years obedient
To one divine intention, from my birth
Preformed within my mind, which by its aim
Made estimable toil obscure and life
Pregnant with issue. This is the intent
That now this people menaces to foil,

Who heed not justice and truth-childed law,
The form of things imperishable in act.
But only this is worthy of us two,
For we of Rome are worthy; other ends,
This creed of gods more foully made by man
Than man himself, the service of our flesh
That to corruption hastes, authority
And wealth that with their surfeit burden us
Ere time usurps them, such trusts and desires
Are but the titles of death's usury
Which in the being of his naked slaves
He will exact. But we will build our souls
Into the lasting edifice of states
By molding deathless order and survive
The death of being in the life of men
Which without us were hazardous. We go
Forth to achieve the unperfected world
And set the flourish on activity
By the atonement of its warring hordes
Under one law and purpose, to subdue
Barbarian passion, havoc and wild war
To extirpate, and malice to avenge.
Ours is the mission of maternal Rome
Who in the backward age with treachery
Contended like the savage, but evolved
Into slow harmony until she bred
Caesar, the only god that has availed,
And with him law, the birth of happiness.
Now in her self-wrought unity and power
Rome will convey seeds of felicity,
Her image and her beatific sway

Imperial, to the unregenerate swarms
And turbulent of the apprentice world.
So to inhospitable coasts her ships
Her legions to the wilderness bring law
And peace to all men till the width of earth
Become one Rome, one empire with one root
Bearing the world upon its myriad boughs,
Dividing discords, and the severed parts
Nourishing in their stations. This to found
War yet retains short lease that Roman steel
May first compel the law and minister
To the reluctant provinces their ease;
Bloody beginnings work to prosperous ends
If the blood shed be evil, since all good
Only by warring over evil grasps
Its destined victory. That visioned end
Is the companion of my nights and days
And soul of effort; but this passionate
And headstrong people, Israel, in trust
Of Caesar here committed to my rule,
Threatens the world's tranquillity; its God
Commands withdrawal from man's brotherhood
And the municipality of states,
Of whom but this I know to honor him
That you do honor him. This late unrest
Between their council and this sudden seer
Portends to Caesar's sway another check;
Men say that he is good, but good must grow
By Rome or never, and my heart is sore
That in my charge alone Caesar must yield."

Then Claudia: "Pilate, for these designs,
Long known to me and meditated long
In our twin minds, you are to be more dear
Than for your love of me. But the main world,
Whereto we journey, silent lies beyond
The narrow circle of the world we view,
Hemming our life with sense. And thence this night
In troubled sleep I heard a voice, not sprung
As if from sleep, nor rousing as of man,
But dropping with the brightness of its birth
Into life's dimness from a clearer clime
To which our life is all as nebulous
As is our sleep to life. It said to me
That Jesus Christ the Just bestead by foes
Must seek redress of you. If this should come
Unhand you of him for your justice' sake!
If the conjunctures intricate of chance
Should counsel you to wrong for Caesar's sake
Would right prevail or Caesar? Time is like
To press you for election."
                              But he spoke
With patient smile: "Said like a woman, moved
To instant deed by unreflective fear
Or mere desire; but I, who am a man,
Must question impulse for its origin,
And on the motion of unclouded truth
Safely devise. If Caesar's end is just,
Then all is just that pushes Caesar's end,
Which grows not by injustice; fear you not
Harm to the prophet if his cause is just,
For in the eyrie of the Roman bird

Shall be his fastness! Hark you in the street
That nearing tumult, herald of new brawls
And of the harshness that attends, provoked
In us who must compose them!"
                        As he spoke,
Apace and quick-breathed a centurion,
To them upon the rampart hastening,
In silver metal corsed against the sun
Marched and grew golden; and his words came straight:
"Pilate, the Jews have brought the Nazarene
And here command his trial; what the cause
So various is declared that he seems charged
With war against all right." Pilate low-voiced
Said "Ah, my prophetess! Now the good blood
Of noble Tuscany and nobler Rome
Rouses to shield this trembling Jew. Fear not
For Caesar or the right!" And straight he sped.

Down the loud stairway and the windy halls
The fearless Roman came, and with strong step
Strode on the hollow court that dozed agape
Under the drowsing fire of early day;
And from the glittering dust his mailed feet
Clashing struck echoes overhead that rang
Like bells of panic. But where the hooded port
Flung its aggressive arch with bold advance
Into the city of the tribes the crowd
That bore the captive Christ, with various shout
And aimless eagerness to see, now surged
In dubious tumult. He, white prisoner,
Alone beyond the threshold, bound and sad,

Stood with eyes downward, while above his head
The pontiffs from the eminence of their mules
Decreed death with their eyes. As Pilate came
The turmoil ebbed, and furtive eyes grew fixed,
And every ear was turned, while he to them:

"Why run you wilding through the morning streets,
Insensate? If on Roman justice bent
For the offenses of this man, be warned
That justice you shall have; for if you fail
To show some cause of trial then you stand
Yourselves for his arrest and tumult urged
To Rome accountable." (And Annas heard
With anxious frown, for he must push the charge
Before the folk that the folk had upheld
To kindle Roman ire) but Caiaphas
Now took the word: "Pilate, the heaviest charge
And evil the most dire that any man
In other can detect is his: he stands
To the supreme God infidel confessed,
To cheat him sworn of all the wealth he owes
In us, our homage; for he counterfeits
To be the Son of God, who is divine
And worthy of God's honor. These three years
Throughout our bounds with menaces obscure,
And so more dread, and fiendish witchery
And lure of nameless kingdoms he has roved
Tempting the witless folk, and yet contrives
To gather to himself the worship due
To truth divine, and so to carry down
The souls of our whole people with his soul

In single ruin. For this crime confessed
By him we pray Rome's implement to mete
Huge vengeance unto perfidy so huge,
And, in the names of Rome and Israel,
To manifest remorseless enmity
To rebels from the right."
                              A murmur fierce
Ruffled the throng and swelled like a long surge
That shakes the silence with low furtive roar
And headlong onset in a moonlit cove,
Then with spring leonine and sudden howl
With seething breast falls on the prostrate rocks
And rears its fiery mane, but to reel back
Groaning and vanquished to the ocean's cave.
Pilate stood mute awhile and weighed the mind
That nourished each retort, and in the tongue
Of Caiaphas the semblance dim descried
Of flattery with disdain, of threat with ire,
Of sleight with resolution to defeat,
Yet stayed to show his passion lest surmise
Should prove of fear begotten, nor of truth
The image cast. Thus violent within
He spoke mild words:
                        "Rome, mightiest of things,
Is not almighty, tends not nor commands
But those that own her sway. Israel's God
I find not in Olympus, nor of Rome
The chosen tutelary; nay, yourselves
Deny his league with Caesar or his lot
With those majestic phantoms that our minds
Godlike have made in image of themselves

That only to their likes they may submit.
So when the solemn gods in session meet
In haughty council on the fate of Rome,
And with disdainful love, strength-born caprice
Rule all our enterprise, then we but bear
Our nature's own awards on its own deeds,
And all endure with fear but with no groan
Endure. Thus are the Romans to themselves
Most true when they obey the gods, and you
To Rome when you obey her law. Not there,
Nor in the mind of Roman is your God;
Nor find I in your captive to chastise
Because he has forsworn your God."

                                      So he;
But single-voiced the throng uttered one long
And threatening howl, and forthwith Caiaphas,
Fluttering with swelling choler all his robes,
In gusty utterance through his hedging beard
Rage-flushed made answer: "O presumptuous,
Are you the god at whose caprice and scorn
We take our fate? How long must we endure
The chiding of your masked mockery
Who bow us but to Caesar nor admit
Contempt above his orders? Will the pledge
Of the High Council of this ancient state
Fulfil not the due witness of Christ's guilt?
Or must we call an angel from the deep
And windy silence of the secret skies,
Or the High God invoke to certify
Our truth? Nay, trust he not the Sanhedrin,
No man will credit angels or believe

That God has other voice." Pilate still calm
Replied: "I find not in him to condemn;
If you have knowledge of his felony
By your law, have you not tribunals too,
Advocates, judges, gear for punishment,
Rome's pleasure in your will? Take him then you
And judge him, nor demand service of me
That I may not fulfil!" But as once more
The throng grew quick with clamor and unrest
Annas to Caiaphas spoke secret words:
"Caiaphas, now commit the thing to me;
I guess the argument invincible
That will entice and trammel fast his will;
For if he worships Rome but scorns her gods
Then this man's god is Caesar." And as ebbed
The uproar of the crowd to Pilate turned
He spoke with mien of prudence:
                                        "Pilate, lord,
Supreme iniquity by power supreme
Must needs be equaled, nor within our land
Lives there but yours an arm endowed to part
Life from the living, banish man from man;
Nature and law name you the arbiter
Of his deserts whose will has uttered once
Firm the main treason. And to every power
Is ever the main treason; Caesar stands
Dared equally by Christ's revolt from God;
For Christ's profession to God's fellowship
Proclaims him frank pretender to the throne
Of the large world; therefore he styles him king.
The whole world is the prey of kingly minds

Nor holds two with its peace; these warrior hearts
Hold nought achieved while one defiance stands,
But feed desire on each new victory
And for the highest hold their utmost bolt. ·
For from the lust of glory and its bonds
(They know it well) no easing liberty
Is won but by destruction of the powers
That menace its frustration and therewith
Of opportunity to covet more.
And while he strives with Caesar we must groan,
For to declare him of the conquered ground
He will be moved to trample it, and so
Proving us weak to prove his prevalence.
Rulers who doubt their sway will soon impose
Harshly its exercise to solve the doubt,
And thus advertisement of valor shows
But fear, and wanton cruelty feebleness.
Yet those made feebler by blind chance must bear
The blows of her unworthy favorites.
The uncrowned king is all men's enemy,
Trampling the low the better to find stance
To grip the great kings on their pedestals
And topple them for his ascent. And here
Stands the uncrowned, O never to be crowned
If you are faithful! Yours is to elect,
Yours only, if the heavenly rights withstand
By which secure all men bestride the earth,
Or totter at the threat of ravening greed
Loosed with Christ's life; Caesar and Israel
And the blind millions of the uncouth world,
Who look for safeguard from the peril unseen

To those who see and can destroy, to you
Look now with single supplication. Yield
Their safety to the law they have decreed
To weld that safety, and you must forego
Forever Caesar's love and Israel's
And bide reproach from unforgetful minds
Of generations, heirs to Christ's unrest."

With downward and deliberative gaze
Heard Pilate, then upon the prisoner
With troubled query glanced, all unaware
Of faces stern with agony of hate
As with the pang of beauty, or the eyes
Of Annas gloomed by reverential lids
Suppressing triumph; but he as in dream
Spoke loud his thought: "Uncrowned, all but unclothed!
There is no beauty here nor comeliness,
But aspect of a leper and of one
Struck and afflicted; yet I see the king
Carved in his silence and proud tolerance;
Silence has more of valor than loud deed
If it be not of fear; this Jew has learned
To act the Roman and if the will be thwart
May lightly peril that he images.
Come, I will question him! Let him be led
Behind me to my closet!"
                                        So he strode
Into a narrow armory that gave
Upon the court. No morning entered there
Save one dull gleam that, straying through a grate,
Hung stagnant in the cool dust of the air.

Or lay in sheen on mail, or blades of swords,
Or javelins, or many a weapon ranked,
Feigning the legion by their discipline;
Thither two soldiers following led Christ
And loosed him and withdrew. But Pilate sat
And silent brooded on the face of Christ
That in the midday dusk swam like a moon
Inscrutable and boding, and betimes
Marveled that there such stillness of the soul
Could constant stand with so precarious fate
And instant threat; then, to entice the soul
To strip its secret strength, inquisitively
He probed with eager words: "Are you indeed
King of the Jews?" But straight his ears were chid
With accents unawaited, pleading not,
But undefiant, lamentable: "Friend,
Ask of your questing soul if its intent
Be only truth and to accept the bonds
Of knowledge, or to lure rather a sign
Ambiguous that you may make it cause
To pleasure those you rule!" Pilate recoiled,
Then up and eagerly to Christ he strolled
To read upon the face what desperate whim
Moved speech thus singular, that unabashed
Constrained him to acknowledge an intent
That he desired to know not; there discerned
Nor supplication he nor challenge armed,
But only knowledge in immobile flame
That lit the dark and secret purposes,
Penetrative, of his own striving mind,
Striving to know its good; but, with that deep

Apocalypse of his own being blent
He saw live pity, and, to rage turned straight,
Made heated answer:
                    "Slave, am I a Jew
To brook of you question of my good faith
As brook your boasted liegemen? Know my strength,
Who am the sickle of the emperor
And hold you in my orb to hew your limbs
At will, or spare you for an effigy
Of moon-born aspiration for the mirth
And terror of your fellows! Must you prove
The gods first blind their victims? Slough your sight
Of its deliberate mists that to a mist
Dissolve all truth but your own faculty,
Then steal its truth by showing it supreme!
So have you long contrived, until your mind
Is now the stronghold of your lunacy,
Impregnable to truth and wholly bound
To pity of those who deem their power firm
Against your arm. The legions with their steel
Stride through your airy battlements, fancy
Removes not from your feet the galling chain,
No thought or prayer can dissipate the real
Of Rome's wide, adamantine monarchy
Or of your own subjection; pity alone,
Before your mind that abdicates the truth,
Dwindles for you in those who shun the man
That arrogates monopoly and flouts
Alone of all observers the august
Of my authority by deeming me
Worth the compassion of so mean as you.

O, did I yield to weakness who am strong
Or such a stranger were to quiet gait
As are the barbarous princes, I could find
To scourge you for your pity and display
To your own sense your weakness. But to end!
Forget me and attend yourself; reply
Enough take to your question: I demand
Account of you, as by my office bound,
If what your countrymen contend has grounds
That you would be a king; what have you done?"

So Pilate made evasion of reply
Serve for reply in terror of the truth,
Calling his fear disdain. But as he whist
The spirit stood erect in Jesus' eyes,
And, as supreme acknowledging the power
By him committed, with slow voice and stern
Of certain knowledge whelming the mind's dissent
He these declared:
                              "To your authority
Honor, and to your question I am king
Though not of this world. See, the kings of earth
Have those who will defend them: I have none,
But come to men as one by nature framed
For sacrifice, to take their absolute will
As it were God's. I am the first of things,
Intelligence; my everlasting realm
Far from the visitations of the sun
And the fixed change that is time's governor
Resides. There neither any night nor noon
Has sway, but knowledge full that lulls desire

To quiet at its home is to each mind
Its own intrinsic day unwavering,
And calls up in the being of the mind
Its own sufficient world; all spirits there
Live wakeful with excess of their own light
Which is the view of God. My heritage
Sets me with the eternal; neither death,
Nor change, nor time, nor matter can fulfil
Subjects of incorruptible sovereignty."

But Pilate murmured: "An outlandish tale,
Yet if it be the issue of desire
It still fulfils it and persuades belief
Rather than the corrupt divinity
Of Jove whose overlordship we affect.
Gods that the fervor of the Attic song
Commends are but illusions of the race
That song makes maniac, and to the truth
Of Roman sense dissolve into the forms,
Created by the mind, of the mind's law.
But your unbodied kingdom of the dead
Resembles truth and equals destiny
With human nobleness. Is it the use,
Experienced long, of delving to deceit
In all assurance of the afterlife
That leaves me skeptic of your evidence?
Or that you claim the kin of the Divine
Though weak as Jove is foolish and in act
To be destroyed? But neither this decides
My judgment for delusion; for you tell
Strange things with confidence as one whose mind

Was never stranger to them, but aware
Made by the instant vision. If deceit
Dictates your words then it can simulate
In its ally assured authority
As cogent as the very truth of being;
For now at some Chaldaic in your speech
Or at the incantation of your eyes
Strengthens this bodiless reality
And rivals with its likelihood the earth.
Come, further tidings! Though it be to yield
A moment to the mad, reckless to pass
The port of swoon, forsake the sense, be one
With the uncertain progeny of thought,
Drain being of itself, I will yet learn:
Why do you quit your kingdom for this grief?
Why are you born, having so richly lived?
Bethink you of an answer somewhat true,
Nor show too soon your wiles!" So Pilate paused
In simulated scorn, veil of young faith;
And Jesus said: "My subjects needed me."
But Pilate said: "Who are your subjects here?"
And Jesus said: "The spirits of all men."
But Pilate said: "Of what are they in need?"
And Jesus said: "Of witness to the truth."
But Pilate said: "Where is your witness found?"
And Jesus said: "I witness to myself."
Then Pilate said: "You have observed our law
Inviolate in all your purposes,
But what shall I declare you? If no more
Than man, then man unrighteous, for I judge
False your pretensions and release to roam

A cozener pernicious. But if more,
Then we are bound your servants and the Jews,
And I forswear my office and my oath
To Caesar; yet to gain what grander state,
Or what superior duty to discharge?
Prefer to homage of my visible lord
Allegiance to fantastic deity
I may not, and the realm of your report
Fulfils so our insatiable desire
Of a contentment undefectible
That it but argues to the foretaste feigned
Of the desire it feeds. Yet this same power
To satisfy all craving may reveal
Its necessary truth, unless the will
Be made to seek a fiction. And, if true,
This is the very grammar of desire,
Terms of our hopeless hope, significance
To nature's uproar, though to us the mock
Of all our effort who, thus herited,
Fritter the time with baubles and with prayers
To keep our nursery; who would not spurn
This world for yours, if yours be with the truth?
But if you are with truth, must not who seek
To stand with you contest the rights of God
Against the usurpation that the greed
Of men for freedom unconditional
And absolute authority excites?
Will not the rulers of the earth attack
The followers of any law but theirs,
Your followers, and make them as you are
On earth to gain your glory, friend-betrayed,

The laughter of the commons, naked, bruised,
Unpropertied, rejected, dispossessed
Of civic privilege, harried by hate
Even to the grudge of their tormented being?
Nay, but by witching lies to lure to this,
Which is the loss of all if you are false,
Were triumph for the enemies of man
And endless malediction on your head
Who cheat your people of their sole content.
You, resolute to shatter the young world,
To trade vain promises for human lives,
Proscribing all attainment, or endowed
For our deliverance from the bonds of time,
From warning of frustration and despair
Unquenchable but by forgetfulness,
To destiny immortal and the proud
Perception that we are not great in vain,
Restorer or destroyer of delight,
Shall you be slain lest the world fall in shards
Or spared lest it endure? Yet when I pore
Upon your mute and meditating power
Or hear your candid words, you seem to me
Adept of truth and foreigner to doubt,
And no misgiving halts me from release,
To which my function and the law oblige.
But in a mesh of strange captivity
I am to you now tethered, nor can part
My reason, unregretful, from the source
So credible of knowledge so desired.
Teach me to clench with truth the argument
That secretly and ceaselessly my mind

Afflicts unanswered: To what purpose we,
Constrained by law not ours, whither intends
The justice of this world, whither tend we
Who by that justice die victorious,
To what unaging crowns? Too little yet
You have unfolded, nor my mind can grasp
Its lasting peace until its guide is truth
Confirming knowledge. Son of David King,
Though to a title more august the heir,
Strange traveler from the world's original,
Who are you? What is truth?"
       But as he ceased
The silver eagle of the legion flung
Across the slit from which the grey light dripped
A dazzling beam of strong, victorious day,
That straight provoked his eye to the royal wings
And the earth-conquering spurs. With fear agaze
And sudden marveling he stood like stone,
The eagle's lord, trembling to be its prey,
Then with harsh thrust of hand put Christ aside
And resolute went out. And Jesus mourned
And knew frustration, the next agony
In God's decrees.
      But Pilate strode nor swerved
With dull and lifeless eyes that veiled his strife
Past the triumphant eagle and the stark
Lines of the legion to the frequent arch
Where the low murmurous anger held in rein
Scarce by the slayer throng sank to a hush
Of more determined menace while he said
Briefly: "I find no cause in him." And straight

The multitude, with single voice of curse
Roaring, plunged toward him, and a moment seemed
Faces awry with hate and clutching hands
To rise in act to seize, until the steel
Of Rome beat back the frenzied, and the din
Swelled dying on the verges of the throng.
Then Caiaphas, waxing with rage more great
Upon the eyes than human, forward bowed
His wrath-flushed face and flaming eyes and arms
Indicting, and, the last refrain of speech
Abjuring, over-roared the clamorous strife:

"Still overweening, still presumptuous,
Acting the absolute, usurping sway
Where Rome withholds, contemptuous of us
Who hold our charter from the birth of things,
You self-crowned king and solitary thrall
Of your imagined scepter, still as ever
Conceit of power swells your hardihood,
Pricks you to plume your pride-born courage. Nay,
You must be taught, my Pilate, so, appraised
That to be Roman means not to be Rome,
You may display the real in the brave
That, windy, now lifts you to prowess. Know
You are not here to judge but to condemn,
For judgment, by the ruling of your lord,
Tiberius, committed to our hands,
Is since fulfilled; yours but to execute
Our pondered sentence. Should the whisper stroke
The ear of Caesar that his ordinance
Is by your deed revoked, think you that he

Would brook your further life? But, Gentile dog,
No whisper but one thunder many-voiced
From every Jewish throat, denouncing you
Shall shake the Roman forum, if you shield
Our enemy, and you shall know too late
Your master in the Jew. Not even ourselves
First judged his cause, but time and public truth;
For it is famous how he spreads unrest
Down from his native Galilee through all
Countries between the Jordan and the sea
Even to this heart of Juda, sowing men
With thoughts that to their hands grow roots for swords
Of insurrection to incarnadine
Their points within our breasts, Israel's breasts
And Rome's. If murder be the perfect fruit
Of his endeavor (and, it is assured,
He fosters treason), then is nature judge
That he is worth the death. Wherefore despatch
His wages, or take yours!"
                              These Caiaphas.
But Pilate answered eager with clear eyes
As of relieved anguish: "If he be,
As you declare him, Galilean, then
The judgment is to Herod. Take him hence
To his own lord of Galilee!" But Annas
Swiftly demanded: "Do you then consent
That Herod execute his sentence straight?"
And Pilate, disregarding violently
The dialectic of the secret mind
That cast disquiet up to the clear sense,
Easily answered: "What to Herod seems

Let him perform freely for me"; then turned
And to a pair of soldiers said: "Fetch here
The prisoner and lead him hence; but, mark,
See that he goes unscathed!" But Annas spoke
To Caiaphas: "Now is our end assured,
For Herod is a straw."
                              So once again
Jesus came forth between his guards, still bowed,
Still silent, still unhesitant, and sank
Into the crowd, who with no mockery
But deadlier oaths to spoil him of his life
Declaring gathered round him with fixed glance;
Then, quiet with the held intensity
Of bloody purpose, wheeling, while their tramp
Conquered the fluttering murmur of their vows
And seemed to shake the ground, the multitude,
Pressing their eager steps against the sloth
Of mass, straining sought Herod in the rear
Of Christ devoted. And as a tempest fierce
Inhabiting a tumult of swart clouds
Lifts from a wasted pasturage with shouts
Of unappeased ire and shafts of death
And into happy distance bears its doom
Inexorable, ruin to new fields,
In dying thunder, so departing they
Grew shadowy on the streets and on the wind
Dwindled their clamor.
                              So the gate was cleared.
But in the eyes of Pilate stayed the storm;
Who murmured to himself: "Never my arm,
Lord Caesar's deputy, shall hurt his fame

By deed unjust nor suffer Christ to die,"
Yet glimpsed the traitor in his hidden heart
And knew himself divided. And his soul,
By rival counsels hard solicited
On this side and on that, as stern and strong
As separate wills imperious, melted with fear
To weigh the fruit of choice. His will was fate
To the Eternal who had cast on it
The destiny of some all-fateful cause
That should prevail or bury in its fall
The glory of Rome's prowess and his own
And all the hopes of man. Marmoreal thus,
Ravaged in soul by forces more than man,
He hung at poise, nor heeded how the girls
That bore their water-ewers with soft hands
Home from the reedy wells were stricken mute
By looking on his pale, enchanted face
Which told a soul in dim and elfin strife
Locked from the gross earth far, that erst was wont
But to regard the works of hands and war
Corporeal. At last with listless words
"My arm for Caesar's sake will cover Christ"
He went within, amazed at his unrest.

HEROD OF Juda, the unsceptered king,
In swoon of contemplation and alone
Lay in his chamber under night august,
That there abashed the morning with its frown
And held it at its twilight. But a hush
As of a listening choir in suspense
Deadened the wayward wind and purr of heat
And bound the lips of echo. Crickets drowsed;
Grey, limber mouse crouched bright-eyed in her chink;
Close on the arras where the dead flies swayed,
The winter-slain, the live now clung in trance
Nor heeded moth nor spider; straight the flame
And frozen burned of the lamp; the hound at foot
With earnest gaze held fast his lord; the smile
Of the stone sphinx assumed a subtle pulse,
Her feet an eager tautness as in act
To rise from the stone seat; foreboded all
Intrusion perilous. But Herod lay
Quiet as marble on his marble seat

And dangled on his meager neck his head,
And heeded not the omens. For his ghost,
Aching with dispossession of his crown
And the dishonor of his servile ease,
Had sought retreat in the remembered years
When in Judea ruled his dynasty,
Supposititious deity, supreme.
Fantastic now he reigned in the lost realm,
From time's betrayals and the craft secure
Of enviers, immortal made by death,
Forever changeless with the changeless past
And true forever. To his charmed regard
Once more the power of his ancestors
Quickened with youth, and summoned from the soil,
Lapped in the festal mists of memory,
Arrogant fortresses and soaring towers
And palaces of seemly porphyry,
Until the whole Judean land revived
The pomp of ruined Babylon. Once more
Sale of the empire paramount of the earth
Hung in suspense upon a Herod's terms.
Once more he breathed defiance unrebuked
To God and man and nature and reversed
Law by his single breach, or at caprice
Nourished or spoiled the poor, ravished, caressed,
Honored or slew, while crime and clemency
Won equal praise and equal gratitude
For being kingly. And the haughty dream
By its delightfulness to semblance turned
Of the live instant, and, abolishing

Swift the estate of being, moved the seer
Ecstatic of his conquest vaporous
To vaunt, and with great gladness in his shout
To summon: "Ho, my company, to me!"

Then shaken were the skirted tapestries
With furtive zest and forth from the slant verge
Floated a rout of shadowy shapes that hung
Grey-shifted on the tenuous air or bore
In cloudy phalanx swift on Herod's head
And swift recoiled, blank, solemn visages
Like sculpture unperfected. Herod stooped
With sudden tenseness forward, with the sweat
Bright on his fevered brow, and dim discerned
Calm and accusing shades, the mortal masks
Of queens and heroes cheated of their lives
Of old to build his dynasty superb.
There came the mournful mother, Cypros, stoled
In weeds of raven grain, slaughtered at will
Of her own son barbaric, pitiless,
And the three princes, sons of him that slew,
Unwilling by their father's arm cut off,
Lamenting now with clenched and muted lips
Stolen the bloom and ardor of their youth,
The sweets of marriage, hopes of famous power,
And all their fatal prowess; there the three
Children of Machabaeus, formidable
Suitors for vengeance, came, the pontiff doomed
With all his counselors in judgment ranged,
He from whose limbs the rods of lictors scourged

The shrieking spirit, and his kinswoman,
Fair Mariamne, pierced for love of life
To death betwixt her supplicating arms
By her fell consort; and at Herod's hand
The infants slain of Rama with staid eyes
Unsmiling bent their bloody breasts to him.
Then as about the hall eddied this smoke
Of hosting shades one started from the host
And swept to Herod's ear and weakly shrilled
With sighful hiss like a west wind that, caught
Amongst the crannies and the channels blind
And towers and parapets of some wide keep,
Grows hoarse and syllabled: "We are the deeds
Whose column is the column memorial
Of all your kin to all the years unborn.
This day it shall be crested with the last
Crime of the Herods when you shall destroy
Him of all those beneath your roof who most
Is for your thrift, whose wisdom and whose love
Are yours at will to borrow; afterward
Then you shall sink." But Herod turned and groaned
To know the Baptist's features ere the form,
One instant sharp, slipped into the deep air,
And suddenly the hall's wide hollowness
And all the causeways of the light were clear
And sun-bearing; but Herod yet withheld
His ravings not: "You owls of the soul's night,
Take to your damned nests your dismal horns
And hooted emptiness that the false wit
Interprets prophecy! Craven not I
To body in belief wraiths of my fears

And call them embryo. Ho, Hermio!
To me, my court, my court! Hermio, I say."

Straight gloomed the threshold and apace there came
One in a pard's fell hooded, clad beneath
In sleekest silk, an Ethiopian
Of grave and moded aspect. Herod straight
Cried with uneasy gladness: "Hermio,
Welcome today for news of her you serve,
The fair Herodias, but welcome more
Than commonly! You heard me call?" But he:
"Nay, lord, but to apprise you of affairs
Of sudden growth I come: Pressing our gates
Now stand the horde of Jewry and the priests
Bearing amid them Jesus Christ, the sage,
With warrant for his death to execute
From Roman Pilate, if you should consent;
This they demand of you with horrid shouts
Lascivious that roar upon your towers
And threat the bonds of law." And Herod heard
With sudden cunning and anxiety
Upon his face and said: "I have had dreams,
Born of the fuming mists of midnight wine,
Dreams necromantic, fancy's ectoforms
That in a demon-charmed slumber grew
In my belief to real, and I seemed
To call your hand to aid as it is wont
To be alike my lady's and the sword's;
Now you have slain these phantoms with a word,
Unmasked the spurious presage of their words
And their untruth of being, by your mere

Assurance of my cry inaudible
Save to the childing sense. But, Hermio, hold!
You hear the stories of this Nazarene,
How he restores men's health, is full of saws
And all men's lover? Have you heard these tales?"
And Hermio replied: "Men do say these,
But words and men to me are liars all
Until the seen deed speaks their truth of them."
But Herod said: "Not so, the people's voice
Fashions the truth that is their despot's lord,
What though the despot feign by will supreme
To shape the people's utterance; for me
This Nazarene must live! Go, fetch him in
And with him all my court, but let no Jew
Enter to dark our play or whet our brains
To thoughts of blood!"

               And presently began
To stroll through the freaked portal of the hall
In leisured disarray a rout superb,
His followers, with morning flattery
Each on his lips, and in his hidden heart
At the faint roar that swelled around the gates
Stealthy surmise; only the women recked
Not of the tumult who with their lovers came.
These were the clients of the dishonored king
Who comforted with indignation loud
Their master, and themselves with the rewards
Of comforting the rich. Now murmuring
Of promised pleasure they round Herod stood,
As on a shepherd's hut in Attica,
Abandoned on a bosky desert peak,

Cicadas throng, the Muses' officers,
Trolling with ecstasy by art contrived
Their glittering, interminable glee;
So these, to whom betimes led Hermio
Jesus between his guards. But on their steps
Pressed Caiaphas with Annas who thus spoke
With urgency: "Tetrarch, it was ill done
To bar your access to ourselves and truth;
The rabble is for blood; were we not here
Then were your walls bathed in consuming flame,
Rased your slight maniple of guards, yourself
And all your train offered to thirsty clubs
To swig your lives. And these shall be fulfilled,
Despite our prayers, fulfil you not the prayer
Of our vexed people who command of you
Death to the Nazarene for menaces
Against the living body of our law,
Which is the being of our state. Pilate
Is absolute that you comply with them
And straight cut off the traitor."
                                      Herod recoiled
Then with changed face cried: "O, it is royalty
To impetrate of subjects right to live.
Friends, I am robbed of strength, toothless as eft
Though I were tiger-hearted, thinned in force
Of men-at-arms; therefore men come to slay
Me in my frailty, since the hands of kings
Betrayed by subjects to their foes become
Ever unequal. Yet I am forewarned:
Not this way comes the end but by Christ's death;
Good Annas, who by no command of mine

Have found my doors inhospitable, yet
To slay your prisoner demands my pause
And pondering. That Pilate craves, to me
Is feeble motive, who have felt his scorn
And feel it in his present mandate. Ah,
Would I could grip his throat! Annas, forbear
To keep these words in memory; he holds
You in like scorn. You soldiers, what command
Have you of this man from the Governor?"
They said: "That he go scatheless from your house."
Then Herod said: "O friendly devil! Now
My heart and Pilate with the warning noise
Of my divining slumbers are at one.
Friends, I am changed with dreams; heed not those words,
But heed these questions, how the Nazarene
Shall prove his virtue in reply! Captive,
At last you meet a friend, if you declare
With truthful accent that you love me more
Than any man of these; then shall you go
Unharmed for me. Say on, are you my friend?"
But Jesus looked with formidable eyes
Held through his blood-barred cheeks, and spoke no word.

Then Herod said again: "Silent you are
Perhaps to find benignant words; but hear
Another question: Three years have you ranged
The land of Palestine, professing love
To all men, yet you ever counsel them
To abnegation stark of this good world,
To flee by innutritious dim desires
To some far, empty haven of the soul

Where no ill bides for nothing is; you claim
Kingship in this world by no title sealed
Of this world's granting, yet decline to seize
The solid instruments to be a king
That the world offers; you heal the body's hurts
By subtle tricks of leechcraft or dark sleights
(A proper trade for peasants and for you,
A carpenter, to mend now human limbs);
Yet for no lucre, spurning all reward
Save sterile gratitude, your magic you
Implant to grow; power you have and sway
Over the hearts that you have won, and yet
No revenue breed from your conquered slaves,
Abhor the world that gives your power to you,
To you such power is given and despised.
By what insane illusion led or deep
And secret purpose is your mind intent
On chosen destitution and expense
Of unproductive service? Thriftless one,
Why must you live in vain, or how can thrones
Grow but by riches? See, I am kind, and speak!"
But Jesus ever held his moveless eyes
Indicting, terrible, and spoke no word.
Yet Herod said: "Then if you will be mute
Show us your courtesy in some strange sign,
Such as the townsfolk note with rising hair
Or crack their sides to see with jovial hefts.
Clothe Hermio's somber front in noonday milk;
Or fetch the lustrous eyes of some fair girl
Here from her virgin chamber; or dispread,
While droops the eyelid, a deep-laden board

With syrup-swollen fruits from Eastern boughs,
Swart olives, and the moony pomegranate,
And rathripe nectarines and melons tart
And cogitative lotus, for our mirth;
Or draw a spirit from the hoarding earth,
The Baptist's—No, the Baptist said I not;
You did mistake—but call my famous sire.
And for each favor you shall feel our gold,
And wisdom add to knowledge, and go free."

Then shouted all those politicians light
And melancholy worn voluptuaries
"Wonders! We will have wonders!" and for stress
Clustered of wanton whim incontinent
Round the relentless corselets of the guards
To win their way to Jesus and compel
Him to their froward appetite. While these
Jostled undaring with intent unfledged
The Roman escort, and, with clamorous
Unbridled mockery and savage thrusts
Mutual of hands irreverent and gusts
Of shrill lascivious laughter, buffeted
The noon's majestic calm, Herod sat still
With quailing glance; for Jesus held his eyes
Still to the tetrarch's with refusal cold
And condemnation of the tetrarch's soul;
And in those eyes spied Herod his own thoughts
Known and unloved. But Annas sought to quell,
With voice that crashed more than the furious roar
Of winter surf on reefs of the angry north,
The obscene tumult; but regardless they

Struggled and shrieked to win joy's counterfeit,
Till Hermio (and quickly Annas blenched
With jealousy to weigh him) with one word
Struck the throng mute:
                             "Silence, you daws, unhand!
O Herod, when the snake is in the clench
Then prudence is to crush him, not to cast,
Lest the fang grapple the returning foot.
How sleep your valor and your eager sword?
Look out upon this people; it is born
Of a sparse band that, by conjunctures thwart,
Doomed to contend with inimical leagues
And foes embattled, roaring wastes and lands
Inhospitable, girt with cities towered
And bladed warriors, and by this wroth press
Of nature fashioned to close unity
And knit in brotherhood, in time took on
The form of a new nature, pledged by faith
To urge a corporate cause and to subdue
To that particular end. And while their kings
Were of this folk, begotten to the throne
By will of the massed members, then the king's
Intent was one with that of the one state,
And for the single purpose of the good
Of all at once at once all forced at length
Of plight malign and stubborn obstacle
Victorious achievement, striving each
Intensely for the people, confident
Of his own gain in Israel's. Now betrayed,
Ere quenched their consciousness of common bond,
To live and strive for alien nourishment,

They languish and the spur to effort falls;
Exiles from Sion now on Sion's reeds
They hang their songless harps, and with bowed heads
Dream idle-handed of the glory fled
Whose hope had stanched their tears in Babylon.
Herod, you are the king of their desires,
Lives but your valor still to vindicate
The scepter of your father, and to fire
To vengeful purpose their tear-softened breasts
And dying will to battle, thus to take
Boldly the gage of circumstance. And here
Stands the first challenge tendered to the bold,
Ambition's first thin traverse, breakable
By feeblest mettle; here that dream-wrought seer
That would effect the sapping of the lees
Of Juda's ebbing manliness by rash
Assumption of the royal and arrogance
Of power in ghostly kingdoms of the dead.
Thither he charms men's eyes by windy tales
Of grief's emancipation in the glow
Of his God's vision, and begets disdain
Of visible achievement and the aimed
Endeavor of man's toil to conquer earth,
Seducing to inaction puny minds
By giving it the name of vanquished lust
And its reward foreshadowing; or wrests
Allegiance to him from reluctant cowards,
That wish to use their self-authority
To self-appointed ends nor own the need
To do the orders of the king of shades
Still in their fleshly fastness; these he swings

By threats of their survival of the flesh
And in eternal flames anguish supreme
And irremediable. Jesus pleads
Once more the treason of the gods to man,
Who are the thieves of earth, our heritage,
And tender at the term of the void life
A shadow for its purchase. Man must act,
Not suffer; what he conquers is his worth,
The measure of his pride; his wisdom sole
Is to resolve achieving of some feat
That will exhaust his life and for his deeds
Compel immortal envy and renown
Eternal. And for you fate has declared
The feat that must perfect you, O my king,
Even to be the first power in this land;
And for myself my chosen end of life
Is to be champion of your cause by aid
Lent to this people's rescue from their bonds
And failing purpose, and by you with them
Partake possession of a land not mine
By birth, most mine by choice, peopling its slopes
Once more with lion-hearted iron men,
Eager to carve the legend of their love
On the attackers' bodies. This alone
Is hell and penalty of perfidy,
That I should know my purpose tottering
To give once more this nation to the earth
And you its regiment, and therefore know
The future but a vain and barren gift
And to quit life the sole escape from scorn;
But Juda's liberty is perfect wage,

And all my heaven is but to stand in sight
Of risen Sion under the cedar boughs
Where the great cities rise on Lebanon.
Wherefore O Herod, lord, broach the campaign
To mount your throne usurped by slitting swift
Through your frail foremost barrier! Forthwith
(But with what honor and what dearth of pain
Permits the angry ritual; for these
Demands his own high valor) unto Christ
I counsel instant death; it will adorn
The slayer of the Baptist."

                              Hermio these.
But Herod rose agloom with bitter ire
And cried: "That name confirms me. Hermio
With suave entreaty, Annas with harsh threats,
Jesus with port of insolence, you all
Persuade me to one madness. Now I learn
That when the fates would wreak their will of us
They counsel us in many characters,
Mantle the term of the pursuit of doom
With pied and patchwork wisdoms and pledged hopes
To lure us to the essay. This dead John
Invades with torment my tranquillity
And sows revenge by cunning beckonings
To slay his master, that their memories
May scourge me like fell furies all my days
And press me to self-slaying. But prevail
He shall not; I am stronger than my fates
And spurn their honey, their unique machine,
Which but to taste is death, but tasted not
Renders them shiftless. Christ shall live for me

And go, but struck for pride with ignominy.
You prince of all things forfeit to the night,
The night that is no being, advocate
Of wretchedness, bemused ambassador
Of death's pretended empire, say of us
Hereafter that we pushed your candidature
By blazoning it to the universal eye
Abroad in your attire, our gift. A robe,
A royal robe, a pleader's lily robe,
Shall be for you; what more remains to gain
Of your impending triumph and intent
Is for the shadowy cohorts of your realm
Assembling to achieve, or bid your hands,
Tools of the despot of the ghosts, become
Ghosts and a mist, slip gyves, and let you step
Calm to the ghostly. Go, fetch him his robe
That we may worship him!"
                                    Hereto his taunts;
And from the will of the world's Rector sped
The pang of ignominy to Jesus' heart,
As they brought forth a tattered amice white
And hung it on his shoulders, and with bursts
Of revelry, to which desire was cause,
Gazed on his grave unmotion, or devised
Vainly to pierce his silence and his veiled
And secret eyes with queries or commands,
Or plucked his hair, unhindered by the guards
Unpitying. With listless insolence
And scorn-veiled ire at unresisting strength
Insuperable, they twitted Jesus thus,
Probing with sallies of their hands or play

Of two-faced words to make the false outshine
The uttered true. But Jesus with bowed head
Stood still unyielding, still unsuppliant,
Enduring still, and still fixed to endure
The utmost of man's malice and his last
Power for anguish. And as Hermio stood
Afar, aloof, indignant, unseduced,
Looking on Jesus scorned but scorning plaint,
He with his troubled soul tensely conferred:

"O, this is royal quittance; so a king
Mutely disdains his butchers for the firm
Knowledge of the impregnable design
Of inaccessible will. The world is lost,
Not lost the proposition to attain
A world beyond the world, not lost the form,
To which the mind is molded by desire,
Of larger terms of effort in the heights
Of the soul's flight than those that coax the eyes
Of living men, not lost fidelity
Conscious to purpose indefectible
From birth to death to traverse the top stars
And storm eternal cities, loyalty
To self, its law, its self-appointed end
Though but a wraith of will. Is this well done
To barter the one world for fantasies
Majestic, that to the fond outstretched hand
Slide into drift? Folly to doubt it folly;
Yet all the noblest are by nature famed
Perforce to nurse such folly. Did I gain
Juda for Herod should I not beget

Other desires, provoke my nature's bent
For ampler conquests than the monarchy
Of the earth's wealth remunerates, and stand
Hungry, though holder of the universe,
In famine unappeasable? Of old
I think I have but drowned this headstrong lust
With self-persuasion of the near success
Of schemes to raise my king, persuasion strong
That like the wine of Cyprus lifts the joy
That beckons every hope, and lifted this
To feign the infinite. But now the sight
Of kingly dying shakes the unnatural swoon
Of the will which bears on me with spleen awake,
Roaring and ravenous with infinite thirst;
I am beleaguered by the infinite,
The gossamer vision, the impossible,
The more than all, though all be measured by
Whatever reach of concept; infinite
This dream beckons my longing to attain
And ever wrings it baffled; no desire
Appeased is, that leaves one unappeased,
And one is ever frustrate. Is it then
That we are greater than the sum of things,
Since our desires, mightier than the real,
Urge us to step beyond ourselves, to leap
Beyond the term of being, apprehend
The soul-created greatness, specter fell
Of emptiness that slays us as we drown
In emptiness ambitioned? Or is peace
But found in meanness, in suppression stark
Of the high natural throb that moves the heart

Aspiring to the inaccessible
Of zenith? This is nature's perfidy
That at the crown of things man, the sublime,
Issues defeated, unachieved, surpassed
By brutes that slake their appetites. But truth
The most abhorrent yet has rights supreme
Which all our honor is to suffer. Now
Hope is a charlatan, intelligence
A liar for its tidings of a goal
Beyond its evidence, and love that yearns
For fairness absolute over each fair
Beloved, a natural simpleton. No cure
Is for the error of our birth until
We to our parent night return, the blind
And guideless artisan of strands perplexed,
Of doubt and unfulfilment, that to man
Are life; and in the longed-for death of all
Will be the death of weariness. Meanwhile
I must have courage to perfect my life
By my achievement, seizing what the world
Insolvent can assign me for my birth
Of niggard dividend. Now fear has held
My tongue from giving Herod the advice
That will advance him; but the fear of death
Has vanished with the death of hope in life;
Time that drowns hope and sorrow in one flood
In me drowns only sorrow; if its term
For me destines the kingdom for my king
Then be its term today!"
                                        The ribaldry
Chagrined and jaded had declined to gusts

Of irate murmurs. Herod spoke to Christ
Words of dismissal: "Haste you, paper king,
Dumb knight undeeded, sterile, passionless,
To Pilate now; and when your kingdom comes,
As soon it will, remember us not there
Nor meditate your love of us nor call
In haste our spirits to your cloudy seat!"
But Jesus viewed him not, but turned away
And passed between his guards out of the hall
Unyielding, unresisting. Annas then
Said low to Caiaphas: "This fretful jay's
Fateful caprice now takes a fall of us,
But the next fall is Pilate's, and the last
Shall be the Nazarene's; for Pilate bends
Now to my will. Let us begone and act!"
And they went, silent, bitter, but resolved.

Then Hermio to Herod said: "My king,
Though I your only kingdom were, the hour
Enscrolled on time before the first of days
By ageless fate is here, when your wronged house
Must don the plumes of war, eschewing clean
Its noonday dalliance, and give the Jews
Once more their promised land. Christ will be slain
This day, and the redeemer will be sought
In one of valor and high deeds, a king
Who cannot be but you. But ere your flag
Proclaim your right to heaven, and your name
Pipe to the hosting tribes, there lives a foe
Passive within your doors who will undo
Your victory's initials. She it is

Whom though I serve I serve not as a slave,
Tethered to her but by the homage proud
Of my self-swaying spirit to her lord
Who loves her more than being; she it is
Whose ill co-partnership with you has chilled
The loyalty of Israel, whose name
Ruffles the darkness of Perean wilds
Where through the midnight creep incessantly
The scouts of Aretas about the crags
That hold Machaerus and its angry towers
Up through the clouds in session, who at pause
To vow revenge against your battlements
Utter the name 'Herodias.' Even the blow
That gives your body to the eating dust
And your defiant soul unconquerable
Spills on the air is victor of a king
Worthier than a woman's arms. Herod,
I summon you to be yourself, your own,
Your destiny's, which you must seize or yield
Slave to another's. Now the planet Mars
Awaits his earthly idol, to illume
The glory ploughed by Agamemnon's ships,
The highway to the gates of memory
Immortal that the laureled Cyrus rode
And, bull resistless as the thunderbolt,
The great bronze-breasted Assurbanipal,
And all the haunt of the world's conquerors
Whose thought still jerks the heart, for you the last
Of all his chosen. Therefore gain your heart
First of your stolen glories from its thief,
Your lawless mistress, the marauder, ere

You grow the rage of war! Enchanted king,
I counsel you as counseled John the dead,
Dismiss Herodias!"
                    He ceased; and turned
Herod in act to speak with timid ire;
But ere he spoke one started feverously
Forth from the panicked throng, a statured queen
Whose limbs moved with assent of the whole form
As ruled in supple union by such soul
As gives its climbing to the mountain pine;
And from the sullent splendor of her face,
Kindled to wrath yet soft with conscious grief,
But ever undismayed, she spoke in words
Whose gloomy murmur told of deeper storm:

"I am that Herodias who has loved
You to the world's disdain, reproach of crones
That grudge the ardor that is lost to them,
But every lover's goddess. Look on me,
Who am my only argument! My lord,
Forget you the philosophy of love,
That in the bright tradition of the eyes
Of woman from primeval womanhood
Inherited is ever writ, not writ
In any book, nor by the reason pledged
Of truth, nor by the solitary heart?
It is the bargaining of self for self,
The vow abjuring the propriety
Of body and soul and all their claims obtained
On man and things, that the whole heart be free
To purchase its free fellow; it is resolve

To brave the anger of the world disdained
For love of the beloved, to forswear
The right to be the guest of hearts still free
That will not call you master, and deserve,
By gift of self unmortgaged, the supreme
And perfect conquest of a heart unpledged
To any cause but yours; it is possession,
A kingly heritage, alone which gives
Power undivided, worthier a king
Than rule a kingdom of divided hearts;
It is heroic faith with beauty; scorn
Of all but of the proud heart's absolute
Delight, the constitution of the gods,
The essence of the infinite in time.
But if the wonder come to pass on earth
That of two hearts each is the other's world
And intimate being, and the one forsake
Its conquest, then the ruin is more gross,
More lamentable for the starry height
Of the betrayer's fall. Adored lord,
For you are my unique divinity,
Would you be Lucifer? When we were knit,
Each the usurper of the other's being,
Then slumbered time, desire stood at its term,
And whirled the heavenly element of fire
Blithe where had oozed the blood; around the sphere
Of love where a new sovereign sat, new gods
Were born, ours only, from our vital flame
Creating its own masters, and we dwelt
The parents of Olympus. Now would you
Dethrone us for a minion's petulance

Who cannot charge my treason? Would you blot
Our fame heroic destined with the loves
Of tawny Egypt and Mark Antony
To greet eternal ages? Then must I die
Never to see your shame. By the white doves
Of my great mother Aphrodite, who
Conquered the god of arms, prevail I not
Against his image, this frail hand shall snip
My life, my heart, that feeds upon its love.
Herod, my destiny is to unite
Death with the severance of our bond, and now,
As when John shook that bond, you must elect
Between my life and Hermio's."
                                        She paused,
And from her smoldering eyes Herod's enraged
Caught blaze of resolution and he cried:
"Too many words, my lady! Chide me not
By thinking I could quit you, who do grow,
Like music during lulls, to conscious sway
Upon my soul within the intervals
That join harsh deed to deed. Let him speak truth,
Be you my madness, you are all my life
Which perishes with wisdom. Fool, you die,
Who would persuade me to destroy my friends,
Christ, to whose murder at my hands my fall
Was tied by fate, and now my very queen,
Sole relic of a kingdom harpy-snatched,
Of many false sole faithful, that of me
Bereft of my securities, might you
Unanxious make your prey. You are unmasked
For traitor to my scaly eyes long bound,

Unbound at last by you. A sword! A sword!
That I may drain you of your soul!"

                         At once
Spoke Hermio and smiled with mockery:
"Herod, you goose-neck and you goose-hearted,
I love you most now when I tell you truth
And lose your love; yet I have found but now
You are not worth the living for. Take this,
Fashioned by cunning of the Chalybes,
Whose master-strokes have been for you, smite now,
Feign me your enemy and plunge your steel,
Friend to me still, where the left ribs divide,
But cleanly, for address becomes a king!
Now be there ceremony and small blood
And learn in the Ethiopian a man!"
But Herod cried, incensed, "This for your tongue
Of insolence!" and grasped the sword and drove
Into the breast of Hermio with strength
Such that the dripping point beyond the spine
Stood out a palm. And Hermio fell down,
Quitting the bloody steel in Herod's hand,
And with great hefts lay spitting forth his soul
In flakes of gore. Betimes he quiet grew,
Said, on the elbow rising:

                         "Herod, lord,
The Nazarene is gone and none but I
Stayed in this house your friend. O Nazarene,
Soon shall you lie with me for keeping faith
On beds of darkness where the heroes lie
Nor each shall know his bedfellow. We two
Shall ere the close rejoice over our lives

As over perfect things, forged straight and thrust
Warlike each to one aim. Now the inane
Begins of strength, of love, of wealth, of ease,
Care and perplexity, of self; nothing
Is true forever; here the skirts of gloom
Begin to shred my being. Now farewell,
Prosper, my king!"
                Gushed the black blood from lips,
Closed eyelids and the solemn lips were sealed,
The head bent shuddering and sudden sank
Away, and Hermio forgot the irk;
But the brave spirit unappalled went out
To the invisible. And Herod gazed
Long wordless, murmured then: "O Lachesis,
Yours is a spider's web and trammels men;
Now I must sink.—No, no, say he was false!
Display your friendship by denying his!"
They said: "He was most false, my lord, heaven knows!"
And Herod, somewhat quiet, said: "My thanks
For this desired echo. Take him hence
And bury him obscurely, and begone
From me a space!"
                And when the hall was cleared
Beside the drowsing hound with face of fear
He sat and to redeem his soul from doom
Flung headlong its adventurous flight to range
Its lost retreat in the remembered years.

MEANWHILE STOOD Pilate rapt in earnest war
With his own soul: "If I should cleave to
him
And scorn the glory of my heritage,
How dear though unabiding, then what ground
Would still engage that my unfaithfulness
To men would not be prophecy and sire
Of deadlier unfaithfulness in time
To the new master? Can the wounded will
Yielding be ever firm, or can the thoughts
Of love be overcaged nor slip their bars
And backward cross the deep of sacrifice
On wings unstayable to feed the heart
With tidings of its flouted darlings—Rome,
Service and honor, power, obedience,
The lustiness of arms and steeds, the eyes
Of Claudia, Tiberius' love? No, no,
I should be homesick for the earth forsworn
And poised in double perfidy. Undamned

167

May I leave Jesus then and live my lot,
Tyrant perforce by tyranny of chance?
But that were to betray and earn my shame.
Strange that I may not leave because I can;
Were I not free to leave him then no shame
Were in attempt to leave; but since on me,
Heir to supreme self-monarchy, depends
The victory of justice, its defeat
Will only publish that I love it not
Which to disdain is shame. I shall possess
The curse of things or yet possess my own
Unless by composition for his life
I win the freedom to forget him. But
That I should give this sacred head to dust,
This flesh to dogs to rend on the bare plain,
Forbid it heaven! Then let all-pregnant time
Fashion my mind!"
                 And as he heedless gazed
Down from the summit of the keep the sheen
Of the street's dust was speckled at its mouth
With men like sudden motes and flooded soon
And darkly seethed with multitudes as fierce
As locusts swarming from Egyptian drought
Over the fields of Gad. And as they came
Clustering about the fortress gate he heard
His name upon their breath and, with surmise
Of Herod's pitiless declension, strode
Shrinking in soul but with unhalting steps
Straight to the downward way. But in the court,
Hastening to them, with deliberate spleen
He spoke: "Have you not learned, you rabid dogs,

To yield the quarry when the master bids?
You charge Christ with contrivance to pervert
Your own fidelity, nor find I truth
In you nor in him damnable defect,
Nor yet finds Herod, who absolves him sound;
Straight then release!" So he; but all they howled,
And Annas said aside: "Pilate, the rage
Of Juda is in spate; if you free Christ
Then shall it burst its channel and dissolve
The city in sedition." Pilate then
Said with victorious sneer: "O envious
And taught by envy to disguise its sway,
Sedition then must be, for in the keep
Is but Barabbas with his followers,
In fetters for sedition; and this Pasch
I must dismiss the prisoner whom elect
The people. Choose then! Shall Barabbas go
Or Christ?"
                    He paused with eager ear, then faced
Sharply the disobedient throng and cried:
"O men of Israel, it is the time
Of Passover, when I at your desire
Release one felon, and you must elect
Barabbas, rebel, thief of your lives and goods,
Or Christ, your King; weigh well the issue!" These
He said and stood away to wait their voice.
But Annas cried: "O men of Israel,
Not this the issue, but between one foe
Who meddled our security to keep
His own, and one who jeoparded his life
Freely to bruise our state; the one will live

Quiet if no need drives, but Christ will die
Ere he remit one effort to undo
Our prospering. Have you not heard the spite
Relentless that the slaver of his lips
Flung on your governors, on us, on whom
As on the stone that locks the brawny arch,
Authorities, depends your health? Such ill
Nor wished nor spoke Barabbas." And at hand
As Pilate for the answer stood one shout
Sprang from the kindled visages, convulsed
With passionate resolve: "Away with him!
Not this man but Barabbas!" Pilate shook
At instancy that strengthened on the threat
Of its disastrous issue and exclaimed:
"What would you have me do then to your King?"
And with the accent absolute, no more
Of pleading, but command, that nations take
When, conscious of one purpose among all,
Conscious they grow of their chance mastery
Over their masters, casting compromise,
So ravened Israel with clamors now
That rang upon the stones and buffeted
The airy architraves, and chilled all hearts,
And set the hands of unaggressive men
Groping for hilts. As if the Titan gods
Had sprung from fable to their pillaged thrones
Of earth, old earth, their mother, and proclaimed
With irresponsible and reckless voice
Of storms and seas that know not their own rage
Destruction on man's sovereignty; so they
Roared ever "Crucify him!" And, though cried

Pilate the while "What evil has he done
That I should end him? I have found in him
No guilt; see! I will scourge him and dismiss,"
Yet still the uproar swelled, nor heeded they
Nor heard his frenzied pledge. So he sent back
For water and before the multitude
Bathed his hands, who laid their turmoil calm
To hear him and thus heard: "Innocent I
Am of this just man's blood; see you to it!"
And as he spoke his eyes with pleading fixed
On Jesus but the eyes of Jesus met,
Sad as at taking leave of him. A voice
Cried in the crowd: "His blood be on our heads
And on our children's!" and the great throng roared
"We answer for his death."
                              Then from the pits
Of the dim keep Barabbas was unchained,
And, mounting to the court, serried beheld
The sullen multitude; then with great shout
Exultant and with laughter confident
Of an exultant answer, ran to them,
Tossing his shaggy head. But all who heard
Were silent save for curses low, and shrank
All from his onset save for Christ unmoved.
But as Barabbas saw the face of Christ
At hand he suddenly grew dumb and wan
And fled the sun, knowing within his soul
The shame of being honored more than God,
And no man knows his afterward.
                              The time
That heralded the body's agony

Admonished now Christ's mind, and the will turned
Its adamantine act invincible
To front the fatal period. Pilate stood
Remorseful but unyielding, nor without
Hope of fair issue, to his pledge, and spoke
Brief orders to his officer: "Take thongs,
And summon of the brawny northern men
Of the auxiliaries, who know the lash
And to persuade its bite, two who will scourge
Christ in the people's sight! Spare not his cheeks,
Nor brow, nor any part that may be seen!
Puddle him in his blood, that we may seek
The dregs of human pity in these kites,
Or glut their hate with pain! Perhaps his wounds
Will plead with reason, rendered by this hate
Blindfold, to doff its bandage and demand
Life for the manhood wrecked." So he, and turned
Within to hide the torment from his eyes
That yet his thought must bear.
                                        Came presently
Two palehaired sons of those lone forests chill,
Savage as that dread spot where Judas dead
Hung from the haggard bough. These grasped the robe
Of Herod and removed from Jesus' head,
And then the seamless garment that the hands
Of Mary wove when the Almighty's voice
Had called her son, and of those cherished hours,
That fellowship that isled eternity
Amid tumultuous time, she now must count
Mournful the unreturning last. So he
Confronted pitiless and threatening eyes

Stripped to his linen zone, appareled fit
For anguish; but as the flagellants drove
Him inward to the court his pressing step
Drew them behind him to the scourging block
Like beasts reluctant led to the fallow field
For the plough's labor; and unasked he kneeled,
And gave his hands to gyves, and bent his head.
Then took the flayers each his instrument
And felt the fourfold thong and heavy fang
That ended each with cunning to embrace
And to divide the flesh and let the blood.
And now one raised the scourge, and swung, and swept
The spreading ribs with dull report that told
Of pain to the observers and behind
Left bleeding furrows on the flesh that told
Again of pain abiding. One more blow,
Then fell another, till with rhythmic ease
And fateful loyalty to the instant fixed
To strike, the strokes sworn to alternate pact
To jaded ears made undulating song
With blow on blow in moment murderous
Swelling to one relentless march of sound
That harrowed and enthralled. Annas forsworn
Yet on that day when God was whipped by men
Cursed as he looked and muttered to himself:
"This serves no purpose; rather were his end
Sudden and comely, were it but secure."
But straight he started as he saw Christ's eyes
Turn to the searing lashes, and arise
His shoulders to receive them like a load
Desired and gladly borne, as if in pain

He found a solace and refreshment due;
For Annas knew not that the strokes that beat
Before his eyes upon that anvil bruised
Once more wrought man deformed to the lost make
Of the Divine. And as the minutes lapsed
The strong youth of the heroic Son of God
Grew mangled for man's infidelity,
And shoulders, breast, and brow, and tethered arms
Were torn and stained with the redemptive blood
That for all time through the wide earth should flow,
Souls' baptism. Then suddenly he drooped
In swoon and the blows ceased, but no voice cried
For triumph at his fall, but stood the crowd
Stern with divided hearts.
                  Then clamorous
The rugged fellows of the scourgers swarmed
Thick from the inner walls and seized the limbs
Of Jesus prostrate. He to memory dim
Awoke and, still submissive to his task,
Constrained his rended sinews to obey
With horrid effort, and with trembling knees
Shrunken he stood and swayed and shed his blood
On the steel harness of the Roman guards.
There was a hall within the keep, immense
And sordid, where the troops reveled and gamed
Or whirled their controversial blades, a place
Unfriendly where the spider hung its home.
Thither one haled him and with laughter shrill
Cried: "Comrades, he is mild and the great soul
Is ever wrathful; but the gods have sent
To us the god of cowardice, unworth

His reigning in Valhalla, but unworth
Alike this valiant world. He cannot be
Such king as we would serve; then let us make
Such king of him as fits him! Nor can we
Accept his favor; let us then accept
Of him our merriment! Let us seek clothes
To dress him on his throne!" And all the rout
Shouted applause, and some a stool uncouth
Settled, and some fetched ragged habits flung
To rot upon the midden, and with cries
Pulled from the midst a purple mantle, hewn
Long since by Cimbric or Illyrian blade
And cast, bequeathing like the tools of man
Its honor to its lord, now fit attire
To mark one of his own ambition dupe.
Then one of those who sought a diadem
Came on the spiny branches of the thorn
Heaped for the evening's kindling, pondered them
And took and cunningly contrived to weave
A complex hedge that bristled like a camp
With inimical stakes. And, while the rest
Gathered and speechless gazed with sounding breaths
Of expectation keen, he interplashed
The ends and ringwise bound and overarched
With further branches till a mitered shape
Daggered and sturdied by the woodman's craft
Was finished in his hand. Then all returned
With glee upon their lips in eager race
To Jesus who against a column crude
Leaned, like a ruined ship that many nights
A solitary prey to hungry winds

And swirl of surges far in the outer main
Skysweeping, icy, dim, unvisited,
Has agonized, until with masts wrenched free
From clutch of thwarts and riven oar and helm
She wingless swings and ineffectual
In the black trough of waters, offering
To fate, till her proud timbers are dissolved,
Indignant toleration. Him thus spent
They seized and forward dragged and hung the robe
Of rotting purple on his shoulders seared,
And seated him upon the stool, his throne,
And crowned him with his thorns. But when the thorns
Dropped groundward from the sagging forehead, one
Took the horned coronal and with one hand
A sturdy reed up from the littered earth,
And, heedlessly as one that drives a nail
Into dead walls, placed on the brow of Christ
And hammering it firm transfixed the flesh
With the long spines, and in the nerveless hands
Sceptered the reed. So he dishonored sat,
Jesus, the author and finisher of faith,
Of all things, as of them who all now stood
Away and in derision gazed a space.

Then one strode out and shouted "Hail, O King!"
And stooped to see the eyes, but saw not there
Awareness of his taunts; so he in wrath
Spat on the face divine and harshly cried:
"That be my worship to your craven soul!"
And others came and bent their knees and struck

With knuckles to arouse his ire, or scorn
To manifest amid their homage feigned,
Or seized the reed and beat the mitered teeth,
As who should tar with blows a wary dog,
Deeper to rend the flesh; but Christ sat still,
Nor groaned, disdaining notice. So they cried
"Where valor has not lived, here all is dead;
Let us exulting chant the obsequies
Now of our stillborn King!" And all defiled
In narrow column, and around him crowned
Marched slowly and distraught, with laughters brief,
And cries "All hail, O King!" and searing oaths,
And blows and spittle cast upon his head,
And mockery of tribute; like a haunt
Of Maenads who upon a Thracian beach,
Drunken with wine, leap round a dying bull,
Longing to sip the smoking blood, and toss
Their raving tresses, and to tambours wild
Chant songs prophetic and of import dark,
Declared by old tradition to invoke
The spells of Dionysus.
                    Sudden the voice
Of Pilate struck the mockers still and mute:
"Dogs, have you not already had your fill
Of scourgings, or would you too taste the thong?
Rome will as Romans have her servants act,
Nor punish but in measure as by law
Exacted. Take your captive to the arch
That spans the threshold of the northern street
And show him to his people; strip not yet
These trappings from him of your lawless sport,

That may invoke their pity! Go!" He turned,
And they made to obey.

                 Annas meanwhile,
To prop the shaken purpose of the folk
And move them to relentless enmity
That now relented, chided thus: "Infirm
And aged the lion of Juda, that long since
Palsied the strongholds of the ethnic powers,
With roar infederable, but manifests
At the first aspect of his hater's blood
Now treason to his purpose judged and pledged
To spill it! O, you saplings weather-swung,
Have you not known you must have granite hearts
To compass death for Jesus or endure
The final fall of Juda? Let it be
That Pilate harries him beyond our will
Or our restraint, yet if we leave his life
We leave our peril whole. Let us then press
His instant death, thereafter in the same
Hurl of our onset with the implacable
And lion's valor of our ancestry
To spring to our revenge!" With these and like
He heartened them and saw their lips grow taut
With purpose full erect and with regret
For its remission.

                 But in that chastened lull
Sudden upon the flank that verged the walls
Looking on high Bezetha and the north
A summons loud burst forth "Behold the man!"
And with one shock they wheeled and looked on high
Confounded.

        On an arch that spanned the strait
Of pavement Jesus stood laced in his blood,
Bearing the wrap defiled, the thorns and reed,
And all the trophies of his dolorous shame
Imperially bearing; so he towered
Above them, the quick image of their deeds
Unfolded on the skies, indicting them
With testimony incorruptible,
Imploring retribution. And behind
With folded arms stood Pilate and severe
And urgent question in his mien; who thus
Now further spoke: "Behold your King! To you
I bring him to declare to you once more
That he is guiltless found." And wavered some,
But Annas to prevent their tottering wills
Cried: "He is doomed to die; crucify him,
Or from your prince take a defaulter's meed!"
But Pilate cried with a rare wrath: "You plague!
And shall I crucify your King, who stands
For Juda's life?" But with hard words morose
Annas revealed the threat that should convert
Persuasion to coercive force, and said:
"We have no king but Caesar." Pilate then
Dropped weary eyes and to necessity
Imagined yielded some, and said with scorn:
"Take him then you and crucify, if you
Will soil your everlasting memories,
For I condemn none innocent." But straight
Spoke the edged ire of Caiaphas: "Pilate,
Your function is fulfilment of our law
Which here commands his death, for he pretends

To be the Son of God." But Pilate cried:
"And wherefore falsely? Have you got of God
Disclaiming witness? Wherefore falsely? God!
I must learn more." And seizing he led Christ
Out of the people's gaze, as the great host,
Remembering purpose new, remembering
Its ancient sovereignty and present need
Of warlike deeds to triumph, deeds by Christ
Renounced, howled with unveiled and instant threat
"Crucify him!"

                But Pilate stood with Christ,
Shaken with pity less than fear, and spoke:
"Who are you? Quick, speak you no riddles more
But plainly tell your title!" But Christ looked
With alienated eyes where now reproach
Usurped the seat of pity, and was mute.
And Pilate, moved in service of the truth
Eternal to abandon earth's delight,
Unwilling yet to yield delight so dear,
Thus anguished; and in Jesus' obduracy
Contrived to find the culprit of his pain
And stanch for self-contempt. He, goaded thus
By the mind's horror of itself, exclaimed:
"Ah, headstrong, merely to observe the pledge
Of private whim, silent you plunge yourself
Into destruction and in sorrow me
By grudging me your voice. Weigh well the grave
And unreturning issues of your last
Negotiable moment; mine is power
To crucify you or to loose you now,
Which I must forfeit presently." And he

Who underwent the harrowing of God
Godlike, and showed his Being in his wounds,
Replied with bitter love: "Too well you know
Your answer who I am, and that no power
Were yours that were not granted from on high
Where my eternal realm whose life is God
Awaits its Lord." And Pilate shrank in fear
And slowly climbed the steps, for he at last
Knew that he knew not for he would not know,
But wished but half the truth to be and failed
To alter it by wishing.
                So aloft
Alone before the folk he stood and spoke
Lifeless and repetitive words: "This man
Is guiltless and must go." But Annas low
Muttered to Caiaphas: "Now we have shaped
Our moment; this last blow of many foiled
Shall now infallibly prevail. But stay
Your tongue for mine is cunning!" And aloud
He spoke words slow and urgent. "He must die,
For he has made himself a king, and well
You know that he who makes himself a king
Is rebel unto Caesar. Weigh your choice:
If you loose him you are not Caesar's friend;
You stand with Caesar or you stand with him."
And Pilate knew the choice that he had fled
Through many a subterfuge present at last
With final and implacable command,
And those contending counsels, counterposed
Till now about his will, now in conjunct
Shock on its narrow field, each urgently

Demanding his allegiance undelayed;
And for timidity to drive his will
To sacrifice he hung numb in recoil
Till levied by strong Caesar and the past
He Christ forswore. Turning with sunken head
He murmured to his soul recalcitrant:
"The ancient generations tie my will
To them and to their children, for the act
That from the vigor of my fathers dead
Flows through me to the future makes me one
With them and my achievement one with theirs.
What else then is my nature made to love
But that which it is made to benefit,
The glory of my race? Abides not man
Because each man against what is not man
Defends his kind and the heroic one
Is he who wastes himself for human sake?
So if I free this advocate of hopes
And superhuman loyalties, I betray
My own. Nay, though I yet survive with him
The loss of earth I but survive to know
The loss of all that can command my heart,
And my eternal exile. But for him,
Who has no children, nor acknowledges
The parentage of man, death is but change
From the inhospitable and foreign cold
Of earth to native home; he cannot know
That he would have me die before my time
And feel my abolition in my dearth;
Better to profit Rome and render him
A glorious ending and to him most glad.

My sword for Caesar's sake must slay him then."
So he deceived himself, yet his deceit
Knew, while with soft and shadowseeking steps,
Like one that fears a blow, he downward went
Behind Christ's eyes, and like a sleepwalker
Skirting the court crept to the judgment seat
And sat to give the doom.
                Betimes he bade
Christ to be led to him; who presently,
Though spent and bowed and unregarding, stood
Kingly before him in his ribald weeds
As who in the cyclopian hand of chance
Crushed violently treats not to elude
By waiving one high purpose, but endures
Lord of his soul by selling its one thrall,
His flesh, to be its ransom and sole prey
Of the beleaguering evil. Pilate alike
Looked not on him but his own hands distressed
And fever-clasped, and groped for words, and held
Silence a heavy space, then with deep sighs
Panting he mumbled with far elfin voice
Slumbrous and overheard, like a long wind
Wailful at nightfall in a lonely pass,
These: "Not to hurt you were my single will;
But by your people's obdurate demand
Obliged, to which by duty to my lord,
Tiberius, I needs must hearken, now
I sentence you to bear to Calvary
The cross and die thereon, since Israel's wrath
Is hot because he has a king in you.
And if you can remember that the deed

Is his, not mine, perhaps you will forgive
When we shall meet again; but if your mind
Find your fate growing from my will, its root,
Forget me hence nor let that meeting be!
Better to dwindle to a little dust
Than live to know my shame, though shame were one
With service to Rome's empire. Would that I
Could say 'Farewell' to you! But though the wish
Is true some purpose chokes the words. Yet this
I blazon, not to you, but to all men,
That no man ever showed the natural king
Shining through weeds of lowliness like you,
Nor perish so victorious. Now begone
While I remain, if that be to remain
Which is the first of sliding, or to go
Which is to hold unmoved the laureled will.
Go, lictor, fetch the cross, and legend fix
Upon its head: 'Jesus of Nazareth,
King of the Jews,' that all may read his crime
And weigh his country's justice; and let you,
Who stand, attire him in his proper robes
And doff his rags unworthy!" But forthwith
Shrieked Caiaphas: "Not so shall it be writ,
But that he made pretense to be the king
Of Israel, lest we divulge a lie
By lying of his crime!" But Pilate said,
Disdaining him: "You wild and witless beast,
I am your master and your words are wind,
But mine shall stand irrevocable!" Then
As a long, irate murmur, dubious
And timid, swelled from out the throng and died,

But Caiaphas dared no more, Pilate sank back
Contracted, unregarding, selfwithdrawn,
And swoonlike, silent sat and motionless.

Within the nether chambers lay in chains,
Awaiting fit occasion to endure
Their punishment, two captives of the power
Of that Barabbas, who were now to die.
So to a grove beyond the walls a band
Journeyed and hewed three trees and lopped their boughs
And of their stocks, clad in their savage bark,
Shaped them three standards longer than a man
By half his height, and to each stock they set
A crossbeam joined with cunning speed and skill
And driven fast by nails; but on the head
Of one they set a stake to bear the writ
Of Jesus' charge; and straight the lictor led
Them carrying the crosses two by two
Back to the fatal court. Meanwhile his guards
Had rent the tattered purple from Christ's limbs
That bled afresh or the bloodgrappled shreds
Held to them fast and fluttering, and from his head
They drew the clinging thorns and hid his scars
Once more with the seamless garment; but, to taste
In disobedience to his heedless lord
Some sense of unsurrendered power, one set
Slyly the barbed circlet where each thorn
Its former bedding found. And others dragged
The robbers captured of the company
Of false Barabbas fled, forth from the gloom
Of the deep fastness, who now stood amazed

At the day's sudden blaze and multitudes
Of cool, enquiring eyes, two stunted shapes
Now to be shattered for encumbering
Useless the ways of man. One, who discerned
Nor hope nor fear nor life beyond the grave,
Now desperate had sworn to slake revenge
And win some solace in the last of life
By publishing his hatred for his foes
Detestable, these men who slew their kind,
And with retorted boldness and disdain
Gave gaze for gaze. But one stood tremulous,
Avoiding every eye and horrible
With agony of horror, suddenly
Divining nameless perils that abode
Across the threshold of the light of earth,
Which he must pass that day. Now stood each cross,
Demanding victim, menacing and dumb,
And one thief shrieked and one sought a friend's eye,
But Jesus walked unbidden to the tree
And eagerly and with proud triumph grasped
Its stock like a strong weapon; marveled all
How he did fondle it and laid his cheek
Lovingly to the gnarled rind, and passed
Light his solicitous hand across its ridge,
As who should weigh the valor of his blade
Flush with the brink of combat. But the thieves
Stirred not to take their gibbets, till some guards
Bore on them with the roods; and one stood fast
And took the burden cursing, but the next,
The fearful Dismas, shrank and screaming fled
Till held by force and laden.

And compact
Now moved the grave procession on with slow
And massive moment like the sailing earth
That breasts in sleep, nor effort makes nor pause,
The depths that front the onward of its law.
Calm and pitiless, the centurion
Strode foremost and in pretext at his side
A herald with the edict of the charge
And brazen tuba to confound the ears
Of Juda with the tidings that the land
Was shedding its offenders, and the ears
Of times and nations that the world was saved.
Hard on their steps a serried maniple
Succeeded of the sunscarred legionaries,
By mimicry of famous killers shaped
To be their carnal images, who now
Contemptuously drove with butts of spears
A hollow, that crept forward through the swarm
Of eager watchers in the gate, to make
Fit avenue for the doomed. And followed these,
Accomplices of their own ruin, fraught
With crosses which behind them trailed the dust.
One cursed, one wept, but Christ with face composed,
Heedless of all who heeded, turned his mind
From all but the ascension to the cross
And the way's conquest, and with toil each pace
Won from the sullen earth. Behind him strolled
The legion's second power, to maintain
Broad the free space of passage for the doomed
Or these incite to haste. At last the rear
Out from the farthest skirts of the wide press

Drew free, and with a sudden roar the throng
Gathered behind them like a seething wave
And forward surged to find relief from fear
And earnest of immunity by sight
Of other men in agony that spares
Its easy witness. Then, upon the flanks
Of the globed mass, that strained to gather close,
Annas and Caiaphas and all their peers,
Mounted on snowy mules and gravely reined,
With purpose ruled like captains; and their taunts
Embittering and hatred manifest
Kindled the rabble's hatred. Even those bruised,
Rolled earthward by the column's sworded head,
Ploughing the human mass, at that bold speech
Started and struggled up to win the marge
Of the retreating process, till the space
Was clear before the gates and, like a flood
Subsiding through a narrow, at the mouth
Of the thin street the ragged host grew quick
With effort to advance, of obstacle
Impatient, and a while roared up and churned
Till all had won the passage and their zest
Raged into gradual silence.

                        And while Christ
So walked to Calvary, Pilate remained,
Pilate, who to the ages and the powers
Of earth had broached the immitigable law
Of war upon the officers of God,
Their sovereign. He, in solitary seat
Within the hollow court, from his own world
Exiled in heart, for whose sake yet had he

Forsaken heaven, now was wrapped about
With silence and its watchful presences.
But as the mind, stunned by acknowledged fall,
Some apprehension of familiar things
Groped to recover, it beheld itself
Growing to demon longings and deformed.
Here the desire victorious of his power
On earth, victorious over the desire
Rather to reverence the right of God,
Showed futile every hope save only hope
Of the increase of power, and gathered strength
To slay the last of love and to usurp
The mind's possession. Fixed to treat with it,
He stood with sudden cruelty in his eyes
To drive his thralls, but no one saw save where
Brooding his wife looked on him with strange eyes.

MOTHER OF God, mother of man reborn,
Majestic woman, who at the bitter tree
Besought the burden of the motherhood
Of men by immolation of your heart
To bear his pangs whom you had given to them,
And, by his gift of men, spoils of his pain,
To you, received your children to consort
With him, your only son, as you consort,
Remember that award! For here I cry,
Here on the utmost kerf of the world's wall,
These iron bluffs that bar the western sea
Indomitable, and havoc of its storms
Hurl from the quiet lands, in this grey land,
The fierce and faithful, that another wall
Erects against the tempests of the mind
That ever would beguile us or torment
To banish you and him from your estate,
Ourselves, rich only in the servitude
That makes you ours. Here in this land were raised

Your altars first to show the wonder owed
To your untainted making; and its folk
Grew to the likeness of the thing they loved,
Yourself, even to elect the destiny
Of nearness to the cross and the disdain
That visits it, with loss of all delight,
All dignity, all liberty, all wealth,
The property of knowledge, outward grace,
For loyalty to the crucified, then know
Their weakness by the persecutors scorned
When at the conflict's close they rose in scars.
Now by the faithful valor of my race
Which to the highest never was untrue,
Though not all sinless, yet in that devout,
I call on you. How can my lips of clay
Fashion a song divine, unless through you
Made of its burden worthy? Through your prayers
Then, sorrowful, bring forth within my mind
The shape of Jesus crucified and scorned,
Which is the mind's act of becoming Christ
In impact of its knowledge, that transformed
Into your son divine I may declare
With faithful voice your passion which is his
Even to the authors of this alien tongue
Noble, and once the clarion of your fame,
Haply to mind them that your love endures.

First tell me, Mary, of the flinted lane
And winding through the town, that Jesus trod;
Was it not dark that morning? For the walls

Of towering mansions with their galleries
From its two sides usurp the upper air
And with their overarching spans defend
In many a space the stagnant dusk from day.
Here threaded with their helms rippling and swung
By fortune of unequal ground the train
Of armed men and, stumbling with deep breaths
As loud as groans, Christ followed with the thieves;
And at their thresholds stood the citizens
To mock or wonder or compassionate.
But presently a stone that raised its bulk
Half from the level where its base was firm
Still, though disturbed by the incessant wheels,
Repelled his laboring foot, which, downward pressed
Into its vestige by the heavy wood
In vain strove to evade; and overwhelmed
He fell, and on his dismal knowledge came
The peace of darkness. Then the following troop
With blows or more effectual instancy
Incited the loth sense; which, as it burned
Once more upon the face upraised with toil
Betrayed a moment's pleading, till the will
Implacable to suffer, the unseen
Tyrant of Jesus' flesh and of that throng,
Brought back the patient features. But as he climbed
Straining upon one knee and took the weight
Of the relentless cross and all our sins
Once more the senses staggered and the limbs
Sank in the dust, whereon the uncouth wood
Fell battering and sounding; and his guards

Feared for his death and Pilate unobeyed.

Now to revisit the paternal towers
Of Salem in those days of peaceful prayer
Simon, a colonist, had left behind
Tempestuous Cyrene and the care
Of docile bees and kindly household beasts
And passionless the quiet of the fields,
Unvarying, unwearying. He stood
Now in a niche, conspicuous though afraid,
And watched the turbulence, much marveling
At this unwonted Pasch. But they who feared
For Christ's immediate death espying him
Dragged forth with undeniable demands
And bade to bear the cross, and, as he shrank,
They beat with spears, until with pledge and prayer
He won desistance and the gross beams raised,
While Christ before gripped with immobile clench
The lower length of the world-conquering tree
And eagerly compelled his shaking steps.
Simon, inured to loads and undistressed,
Gave ear now to the multitude behind
Bawling with bloody appetite inflamed
By the priests' railing, and to the plaints or oaths
Of the two thieves, and all around divined
The lust of the Roman soldiery to prove
By bruising weaker men their matchless power;
But therewith he beheld before him Christ,
Worn with his labors, yet desirously
Pressing his difficult steps, as if in haste
To rest on the achievement of a task

To others, not to him, beneficent.
And as the mind of Simon heeding these,
Though dimly heeding, struggled to explain
In Christ the confluence of spirits wont
To be dissociate he suddenly
Discerned the deed of Christ even in his pain,
And tidings took of triumph prophesied
And dreams conceived hasting to visible birth
And throb of new life in creation old.
So, filled with gradual shame for the lewd horde,
He, sedulous with understanding awe,
Fastened his gaze on Jesus.
                              But in time
The instant heat meddled the toiling sense
Which died with inward clamor and again
Christ stumbled and lay prone. But as he rose
Forthwith halted the escort and confined
The multitude with barring spears, and some
Led to the shaded wall whereto he leaned
With inward face and limbs that hardly won,
But by command of will inexorable,
From death their shuddering quickness. There at hand
Stood some poor women grouped, not partisans
Nor taught by misery to hate, but moved
By natural love for one oppressed. They, drawn
To succor Jesus, wroth and pitiful
Regarded now the ordeal. And one
Ran to him leaning at the wall and cleansed
His face with linen, but another cried
In tears: "O is this he of whom our ears
Have caught divinest tidings? Never seen

Till now, helpmate of poverty, ally
Of helplessness, must first we see you thus
Mangled by savage hands, and nevermore
See eyes where first the poor discovered love
But in the throes of memory? O Christ,
Woe worth the day that takes you from the earth
And they that take you!" But for answer he,
In pitiful eyes with eyes more pitiful
And care retorted looking, these to them:
"Daughters of Sion, weep no more for me!
My work and woe shall be my monument,
Title to undecaying reign; more hurt
The slaying wreaks the slayer than the slain,
And better is to suffer. Weep for yourselves
And for your little ones, remembering
This patience in your proper agony,
The measure of your people's sin! At hand
Are now the days when you shall mourn to see
Your children perishing before their bloom,
And know extinction on the breaths of you
Moving inexorably, and you shall cry
For refuge to the caverns of the earth
And the deep bosoms of the hollow hills
Which, deaf, must cast your pleadings from their breasts
Unheard, and turn to counselors of despair.
O then take patience from the bitter truth
That, if the time can harass innocence
Thus as you see me now, no lighter woes
Endure must the deserving!" So he invoked
The fatal war and all the ages foiled
That had conspired with God to rear the slow

Splendor of Israel, and to their dazzled minds
Enchanted presage of the disastrous years
Wafted, when the victorious columns crept
From wasted Galilee to assault the heart
Of the devoted race; of Sion fair
Vexed with fraternal feuds and circumscribed
With strange machines, premonitors of death,
Shattered at last and raped, and in her flames
Receiving the adulterous Gentile's foot
Within the untrodden oracle, now void
But by the banished presence and old fame
Forever hallowed; and of the final woe
And dissolution of the lonely pride
Of Israel, who from the first of time
Had warred with worlds to be alone and free
And all had conquered and survived, until
He sold the lifeblood of the Son of God
To gain his right, and won the state forsworn
Extinction, save for the deathless memory
Of inextinguishable valor. No woe
Nor on such glory of man so fell, nor when
Arbaces and his Babylonian spears
Beleaguered the long walls of Ninive
And after many an onset gave to flames
Its angry towers and its bloodbuilded sway
Far spread and for innumerable years,
And in a single conflagration joined
The pyre of the voluptuous king, self-burned
With all his concubines, by that last act
Burning his sordid fame to be renewed
Immortal in heroic fable; then

Perished a city of feebler renown,
Younger by birth than the might of Israel,
Gulfed in its desolate ashes long before.
Meanwhile the soldiery led Christ again
To walk the middle way and bear his cross
Thither where rest was death.

                         But at the gates
Of the inhospitable city he,
Withstanding death by mere resolve to live,
Yet fell once more beneath its instancy.
And sprang the guards, impatient to complete
The march to the deadly hill, upon his form
And with great shouts and haling of his limbs
Quickened the jaded sense. But as he raised
His thorny head and knowledge seized again
The faded eyes, whose were the eyes but yours,
O Mary Mother, that upon them gazed
And anguish gave for anguish? There you stood
Awaiting him with John, bondmaid of love,
Hating what love constrained you to behold.
O who can tell your incomparable woe
At gaze upon the harrowing of your son,
And all his justice and his strength divine
And kingly tenderness to havoc given,
His, who to you was full acknowledged God
And ultimate desire, more than yourself
Who were all lost in him? What heavier blows,
Far heavier than had your own body bruised,
Then fell upon your spirit innocent,
Clamorous with immitigable pain,
When you beheld the scornful crown, the lines

Of whips that wandered on his flesh and dewed
Earth with his blood, and read upon the cross
The fall of all his manhood now decreed
And slow extinction of his life and being
By men bent to erase him from the earth!
You saw; and understood not how your life
Endured, though suffering instant defect
In his destruction who its essence was
By faithful love translated. Did not then
Glimmer between your eyes and his a wraith
Of the delightful years, summed in exchange
Of momentary memory, when your child
Divine, but yet your very own small babe,
Imparadised your penury with his smiles;
Or later when, bearing the heated axe,
He from the cuttings to your hearth strode down
And lit the evening with his gleaming speech
Of simple things known wisely, or was mute,
Moody awhile with musing on his aims,
(How with austere abstraction set the lips
In carven frown bold and solicitous,
Remembered lips, awry and mangled now
By iterated battering!) or when
(Seeing then first what things he always knew)
He looked with you from high-sloped Nazareth
At dawn on trains of treasure-laden beasts
And traders black, charred by the suns of Ind,
Through that dry throat that linked the parts of earth
Pressing with Asia's produce rich, their trove
Of raiment mottled as the varied plumes
Of forest birds, from lost or famous marts

Where common were all wonders, Madian
And Maracanda and Persepolis
And towns forgotten in the Oxus' nooks
And many-citied Ganges where the gems
Retorted emulously the morning's rays
With crescent fire, and golden Colchis, rapt
Dreamer upon the solitary isle
That harvests the marched fields of ocean's pearls,
Taprobana; and as he looked his eyes
Drank eagerly the wealth of many hues
And his lips told you his delight? How he
Rendered you homage glorious the more
For glory of the vassal, and deferred
To you, and comfort took of you, and feigned
All to depend on you, your God! Supreme
Was now your horror for this issue dire
Of such exceeding joy. Must all earth pass
Even its divine? And must an earthly hell
Resent the being of the heavenly fair,
Or need devise a superhuman bliss
With resolution on great agony
To shake the quiet of heroic hearts?
From him you stricken turned, but unsubdued
To turn him, and your tearless, silent face,
All marble-white and hard with anguish, dropped
Upon John's arm and with him bore aside,
Numb with your intimate pang. But he, whose eyes
Now first in many hours had drunk from yours
The love for which he died, felt your love race
Like potent fluid in his veins, and life
Tarry within his members. And he arose

And took once more his freight, and husbanded
His strength, doling its measure to each step
Performed with circumspection, that his eyes
Might close no more but on the dark of death.

So to the destined field the Saviour came
And spent on the achievement of the road
His last of virtue, shrewdly spending it,
Strong steward of himself. For he had willed
There to contest the strife, to which all years
By exercise had trained him, and endure
Inactive there his slaughter, but his end
Unyielding, which to yield alone is fall.
It was a stage inept for feats of pain,
A plain appareled by the diligent spring
As for a festival, where myriad blooms
Usurped barbaric splendors from the sun
And waxed in savage wantonness, erect
And arrogant, pied as the morning dyes;
And in the thorn the sparrow's fitful lisp
Strayed meditative, and the enormous air
Was social with the swallows. There would boys
Rejoice to wander and experience
Ever more warrant of immortal youth
In all the changes of the versatile world,
Which heightened but delight; now lay the place
Confronted with its portent's mockery,
Christ tortured and to die. But in the midst
Uprose a pedestal of somber rock
As high as thrice a man, its flowery foot
Bastioned by bones of perished felons, bleached

By weather and the tongues of famished dogs,
And on the naked brow a naked head
Showed with barbed beak, demanding carrion
With patient presence.
                        Unto this rock accursed
They led the Son of God, untarrying
But spent and slow, and Simon climbed the steps
Hewn in the rock, and on the summit laid
The cross with wonder, and apart withdrew
To grasp the issue. But one legionary
Seized on Christ's shoulders and unheeding dragged
Up the abrasing ridges of the stairs
And laid him trembling, but alive to die,
And mixed an anodyne of wine and myrrh
Which to the lips of Christ he bore. But he,
Jealous to keep the originality
Of his defeat of pain nor suffer men
To deem it wrought by matter's instrument,
Refused his lips and toiled to heave his bones,
Contending silently, until he stood
Once more erect and waiting. And the thieves
Had now achieved the level, while the troops
Below confined the bickering populace
A space from the gaunt hill's flanks; and last there climbed
The fatal peak the killers with their gear
Of nails, and wedges, hammers, ropes, and spades,
To press the siege of God.
                        Contiguous
First to the pits, delved in the rock of old
To base the feet of other stocks of shame,
The butts of the three crosses they disposed,

And the three doomed, each to his gibbet near,
Stripped, but the seamless garment, fast about
The clots of Jesus' lacerated flesh,
Scarce won but with great labor. And he stood
Clad in his linen zone, a spectacle
Of manhood marred, a moment to the throng,
Drooping beneath the searing of the whips
Renewed to sense, and pouring forth his blood.
A moment standing thus they seized him then,
Those killers cold, and hurled him headlong down
Limp on the rugged wood; and one gripped fast
The hand that he desirous stretched along
One arm of the cross, another took the nail
And hammer kneeling, and put point to wrist
And with address swung hammer and struck down
Once; and with rending loud the nail went home,
Jetted the blood, and all the members clenched,
But no cry came save low the words: "Father,
Forgive them for they know not what they do!"
But from another cross, hatred of hurt
Or of the hurters heralding, a howl
Of rage and from another burst a scream
As of a tortured child; meanwhile in foil
Took the world's victim unresisting, mute,
The nails in hands and in each foot a nail
And lay incapable. But in his soul
Was quiet, though the outlawry of God
Was now entire, since, evermore beyond
The last of effort, there he crowned his plan
With his desired torment, and he prayed
That in remuneration for his pain

No man should lose its harvest, though by man
Inflicted, yet in ignorance and way
For the Lord's second conquest of lost man
Affording to his mercy. And forthwith
The sun, that the ethereal pastures bathed
And soaring temples of the air with brisk
And ardent lightnings, niggard of its fires
Became and, a blind orb of blood at gaze,
Loosened the gates of darkness. On the earth
Thickened a purple air illuminous,
Pall of funereal grief; and he who saw,
Pilate's centurion, that mid-day dusk
And Christ's desirous passion, and his prayer
Heard for his torturers, stood rigidly,
Stunned with suspicion dread.

                                   Instructed now
For elevation of the sacrifice
Was the great cross, the instrument by God
Chosen to vanquish the insurgent earth;
And with it dressed the crosses of the thieves
Were ranged. Then, to secure the gripping nails
Against the shocks of raising, with stout cords
They bound the bodies to the roods; and one
On shoulders raised the cross fraught with the form
Of Christ, who shuddered at the fitful jars
Conveyed to the pierced limbs, and one contrived
To guide with ropes the gibbet to its pit,
Where they must wedge it fast and loose the cords
That bound its burden to its breast. And clear
And sudden to the watchers on the plain
Skyward from the black height the cross of Christ

Rose like a mounting sun, his naked breast
Delivering helpless to whatever ill
The world might send, which he had made and now
Would make anew. But the impassioned throng
Saluted with one howl the boding sight
By fear or obdurate defiance moved,
Till the thieves mounting to their stations fixed,
On roods of torment one on each hand of him,
Made hideous with their shrieks the unnatural night;
Chilled then the other clamor died, lest paean
Should pass for pity's speech. And it was noon,
Noon of that day and the whole vast of time.

Now to its term ascends the agony,
Which in the contemplation of my mind
Has robbed it of itself for many years
Or of the visions that my eyes report,
And changed to Christ, fraught with the passionate rood
And all the woes of time. Yet though my soul
Has borne to be abolished with the past
And crucified by peremptory dream,
At point to round the incantation now
And slip the magic of abducting thought
It fears the natural light, where it must dwell
Perplexed, a stranger in an alien land.
Better this life to hang upon the cross,
Wrung with the forms of those world-freeing scars,
Ruined with God incarnate, ceaselessly
Yielding my mind his tabernacle, where
His body and blood, though panged, not glorious,
Liken their knowledge to his sacrament,
Than buy complacence by inhabiting

The thoughts of earth, wherein the greatest thing
Is only man. Where is the pride of earth,
Which has forsworn ambition infinite?
Where is audacity when men are scared
To stake all hope upon an argument,
To follow reason, their one natural guide
Infallible, even to the period
Of quest, though arduous and solitary,
But heed it not, and to eyes' sentence leave
Crisis of the invisible? This world,
Indifferent to the metaphysical tongue
That tells our title to the infinite,
Thus abdicated, soon will be again
Abode and prison. Yet inexorably
Till it be all revealed my dream commands
My voice, and I must speak till all be told,
Though they who hear the dream deem it no more.

Upon the height were raised conspicuous
And impotent now the three stocks of scorn,
Of scorn the aggravation of all pain,
Against the sun sullen and formidable
With warning gloom. On guard beside each cross
Posted, an idle band of legionaries
The slow ascensions of Christ's anguish watched
In act of death's achievement, and their steel
Glowed in the sluggish beams as burning brands
From central fires. And some looked up awhile
Wordless, but one cried: "Now, you fool of fear,
Your throne is more becoming than our block,

Explaining to your braggart race that none
Shall live but who can battle." And the rest
Approved in silence, and a few drew close
To dice for the seamless garment; but apart
Grave and unheeding the centurion stood,
Debating on the meaning of the signs.
Beneath them to the city walls the plain
Spread, and upon its face bore companies
Of gazers, with undeviating eyes
On the cross straining, all with deep unrest
And secret passion moveless. Some were mute,
Some rustled, all repressed their turbulence,
The soldiers under sway of discipline,
With awe the guiltless, some with guilty fear
At the accusing gloom, with triumph most;
For these constrained all forces of their mind
To the one act of savoring at full
A passionate desire achieved, nor knew
The dismal oracle of noon denied
And the attainder of the heavens more
Than armies, locked in fray ambiguous
And fraught with utter hopes, beneath their feet
Attend the earthquake or upon their brows
The instant hail, for exultation wrought
By prowess and the sense of power born
Of slaughtering unscathed. Annas of these
And Caiaphas stood close beneath the rock
With the hieratic college, each by his mule
Stationed immobile, with firm visages
Held high of victory and conscious might,

Which to their eager minds seemed now supreme
While pondered they the pattern manifest
Of vengeance for its slighting.

                           Soon the throng
Began to break. And some because of fear
Importunate crept silent to the walls,
And some because of cruelty appeased
Went from the stricken plain. But as these crossed
The shadow of the rock a legionary,
Moved to persuade their laughter and to feel
Some tribute to his power in their response
To him, the moment's demagogue, cried out:
"If you are true king of the Jews, come down!"
And some laughed furtively and fiercely some
And paused to look again; but one stood forth
To emulate and snatch the mocker's brief
Repute, and thus exclaimed: "O wing-trussed, yes
If you are eagle, snap these tender bonds!
If you are Son of God, descend the cross!
If you have promised to unfound our fane
And sow the leagued fields with the strewn stones
Afar dismembered, and within three days
To resurrect it from the dust, repel
Your own undoing now! But you are proved
And all your promises for fumes of vaunt
Discovered vain. Hang, impotent, unmourned,
Who would dissuade our valor and to chance
Submit us unresisting!" And the crowds,
At gaze expecting the response of Christ
Nor in his silence reading their response,
Strengthened their self-approval for the deed

And took new hardihood, hating him more
For what they deemed the folly of their trust
In him of old. And furiously they seethed
With hands and words, confounded in uproar
Of threats and taunts and vows of enmity
Meddling the torrid air.
                        But Annas saw
In their unpunished insults argument
Of Jesus' weakness to confederate
His fellows to his will in constancy,
And pointing to the crowd addressed the priests.
"Now is the hour that hoists our trampled might,
Invokes us by rich titles, fostersons
Of divine predilection, dignified
By this achievement arduous. This hour,
That manifests our purpose stanch, proclaims
Our first of resurrection, and predicts
The perfect empire seized unrighteously
By strangers if relentless hold our wills,
Which have subdued to our determined end
The folk this day and autocratic Rome
And our reviler Christ. The very folk
Unmask his hollowness, who if he came
From God were now forsaken not of God
Nor helpless bound nor mortal at our hands;
Nay, should he burst his iron ligaments
And even now step from their clinging free
And walk upon the rock, we should believe
His witness. But he boasted to dissolve
The bonds of others and is now declared
By his own overcome, full testimony

That he was false and that we stand by God
In shattering his falsehood and his life
From which it grew. Then blessed be this hour
And worthy of the timbrel and the harp
And solemn ecstasy of dance, that now
Invites to sing the union of our tribe
With its reborn dominion, pledged today
To grow supreme hereafter! But today
No music must extol our victory
Save the still jubilee of the secret mind,
That knows the way to triumph but retains
Privy its high designs, therewith retains
Inviolate the terms of fate. Behold,
Our crown approaches! Let us go from hence
To plan its apprehension!" So he adjured,
Deceiving and deceived; and they gave ear—
With gladdening breasts, but feared to look on Christ
Lest doubt should gnaw their glee. Then, with raised hands
And faces, as with vindication dire
Of justice, stern and menacing, they turned
Their mules behind the shreddings of the throng
And walked them staid as in a liturgy
Slow to the horrent towers.
                                        But aloft
Christ shook the obduracy of hostile hearts
Already by his wounds, and men subdued
Even by the trophies of their victory.
The spirit of the thief who at one hand
Rose hanging, wrung with pain intolerable,
Revolted from the pressure of despair,
Yet found no solace present nor by hope

In man predicted, though devoutly sought,
Not even that desperate ransom of despair,
The hope to win tribute of fear or praise
By his unflinching hatred in defeat.
Hemmed by a hostile universe the mind,
Fierce with its need of hope, prayed to what gods
Might by that need created be to feel
For sake of pity or caprice some strength
Against the whole world's whelming enmity
By witnessing perdition on his foes
Loosed at his sole demand. Cursing all men
With shrieks the thief hung writhing, till his glance
Found Christ, and, prompted by the mocking din,
Exclaimed: "Why not indeed, O cheat revealed,
Since you are Christ save you yourself and us?
Haply they only move your pitying power
Who can repay with service or rich gifts;
But whether void of pity or of power
Curse your futility that now betrays
Those who have trusted in your vaunts, contrived
To lift your greatness and to work our fall!
Hell be your grave!" But on the cross in face
His fellow spoke: "O proud though wholly shamed,
Would that we were together free that I
Might ghost you with a buffet! Insolent,
Defiant of the Almighty, even now,
Even in the roaring of impatient death
Attending to convey you to your trial
And claim the sentence of your deeds, you dare
To harry justice to the last? (O God!
Insufferable this pain, insufferable

Most for its meriting, that drowns the hope
Of all rebate of our everlasting debts
For these revenges!) Mocker unadept,
Because of no man the superior
And most of all debased, he whom you mock
Bears for his kindness unjust agony,
We for our evil penalty deserved;
While we did curse he prayed for those that slew;
We show the natural devil, he the God
Above the natural; here between our breasts
Is one who tops the human, and, in him
Dying, hope's shade rekindles. O Lord Christ,
If there be any substance in man's hope
You have the springs of strength and of all good;
You are what you declare, though I untaught
But guess your title. Now remember me
When to your kingdom you ascend; vouchsafe
Quiet at last after this battering world
That overpowers now my unequal arm!"
So he declared between the gusty sighs
By pain forced from his lips, in fitful speech
Prolonged. And Christ looked with untroubled eyes,
Untroubled though his breath went quick and harsh
To move the laboring heart, and whispered loud:
"Remember you I shall; this day with me
You journey to my home." And the elect
Wondering his unutterable thanks
Showed in his eyes, and straight to silence slipped,
But knew thereafter that his sternest throes
Were but medicinal, and potent more
To change the evil of appearing things

Into the blessed truth than any drug
Of earthly skill to bury it in sleep.

Meanwhile in purpose fixed to stand by Christ
Hardy and heedless of the threats of chance
Came John and Mary to the deadly rock,
With whom two other Marys, Magdalen,
Came, and of Cleophas; and as they climbed
And overpeeped the brow a soldier cried
And made to cast them backward; but forthwith
With peremptory mandate quieted
Him the centurion and strode up to John
To learn his errand. Whom thus John besought:
"Soldier, if any pity has survived
Unslain in you with those your hand has slain,
Now let it waken! She it is, whose eyes
Of human eyes first in the infant Christ
Rejoiced, his mother that implores you here
A last and solitary boon: to cling
Close to his side and take what bitter joy
May be in numbering his dying breaths
And speeding the last offices of love.
Be not against us to desire us hence,
But leave us our poor solace, him to see
Our uttermost devotion, us to feel
His love, and each in each some refuge find
From the harsh tumult of this agony!
Soldier, be gentle!" But the centurion
To Mary turned and silent gazed and long,
Nor harsh nor kindly, but as questioning
With awed and earnest inquest portents strange

That seemed the lucent veils of present power
Unearthly; then abruptly he was seized
With an unwonted grief and with brief words
"Go as you will!" wandered aside to watch
And ponder. But the blessed four went on
And wheeled about the cross and stood in face
Of Jesus hanging; sank with stifled cry
His mother on John's tightening arm, but she
Of Magdala ran with despairing sob
And crouched beneath the rood and with the blood
Endiademed her tawny hair, while limbs
With her abandoned weeping quaked. Above
Jesus looked wide-eyed then with sunken lids
Sighed for fulfilled desire; and in his mind
He saw his mother as his tool of power
At hand, in whom should tarry some of him,
After his passage from the earth, to tend
The tottering footsteps of the new-born Church,
His second self and angel of his truth,
Its mother for a space, therewith to be
God's harbinger to woman and to all
Almoner of his succor. Minded thus
He looked on her with kind authority
And throned her with a word: "Mother, behold
Your son!" and equal bidding gave to John
Regarding: "Son, behold your mother!" Straight
The mother understood and bent her head,
But John heard, wondering at the testament.

So like a monument of ancient grief
Stood Mary by her dying son, nor moved

Her sunken head hid by the falling veil
Nor fingers folded in her robe, but still
And soundless stood, as if with thoughts of him
Her ghost had dogged its thought and left behind
A marble corse unsouled. And at her side
Stood John rapt all in her, through her in Christ,
And by them both Mary of Cleophas
Her sedulous dim-comprehending ruth
Gave and with them was quiet. But at the cross
Tossed Magdalen her desolated breast
And uttered witless words and sobs profound,
Veiled in a shroud of tears, throughout the hours
That heralded the ransom of the world
And the victorious death.
                              But now the dim
Mind of the dying Christ by its decree
Of self-surrender to invading death
Was moved to end its weakening grasp of sense
And, on itself retorted, draw afar
From these outwards, though dear. In that retreat,
The solitary vestibule of death,
The sting of the desires of earth no more
Shook the secluded soul. But one desire,
Which was the guide of all desire and deed,
The thrust of being towards its end divine,
Took new might from its solitariness
And blazed distinguished for the lesser fires
That glimmered on the marge of consciousness,
Quenched as by sleep. This was the will supreme
To gaze forever on the face of God,
Which from his birth had been fulfilled in Christ

And stood between his spirit and distress.
Nay, the extremity of dearth had served
By its denial of inferior hopes
The more to join with undistracted strength
His soul to its supreme possession fast,
And in the vision of the good of God
To turn it to such comprehensive joy
As the control of earth could not increase.
Like to the fabled fount of Ammon where
Warm the wave bubbles in the chill of night
When the swinked sun finds its night's hostelry
Couched in the oozy fund, but when the day
Calls up the sun behind his dazzling steeds
Cold then the waters of the Ammon spring
Mourn for their heavenly emigrant; so the soul
Of Christ amid the gloom of grief had turned
To view his inmost being, which was God,
And in that view touched the acme of bliss
Beyond all bliss denied. But on the cross
Jesus, that he might suffer there for man
Conspicuous torment worth man's total love
And so persuade his heart, retained the sight
Of God, which was the sight of his own being,
But yet forbore to take his joy of it,
Reining his longing will. And the will groped
In vain for its fulfilment nor achieved
Within itself the act of joy supreme,
Which is its incline to its final rest
In its attained desire. Now at its term,
But still incapable to apprehend,
Dire beat the will upon its self-wrought wall,

Imploring of its own fidelity
In vain repeal of its decree, and strove
Against itself divided. Now was borne
Most violent the strife that any soul
Had waged on earth or yet should wage, the head
Of all the sorrows of the Son of God,
Whose strength was patience and the pledge that death
Redeem would the redeemer. O what thought
Of man can penetrate this solitude,
Or can conceive how God could go in quest
Of God and find in vain, or edify
The woe of one that knows God unrejoiced
By inference from intellects that know
Created shadows of divinity
For richest of things seen? Bereft, the mind
Of Christ, though waning to the sleep of death,
Yet cried for the bright vision's lost delight,
And fought in tears captive against the bonds
Of darkness, till the alarum of his lips
Told to the watchers of his agony
At its unearthly peak as the words were hurled
Shattering the quiet tense: "My God! My God!
O why have you forsaken me?" And all
The listeners felt their rising pity numbed
By sudden gust of fear as dim they sensed,
More grisly for its mystery, the form
Supreme and the impenetrable depths
Of that immense of anguish.
                                   Thus the soul
Of Christ still like the lesser heroes held,
Before privation still unterrified,

Its oath to stand fast and repel till doom
Should overbear, though they by feats of arms,
He by the brunt of pain borne unseduced;
But now he must adventure his extreme
Travail, and utter desolation tempt
To win the purple of the heaven and earth
And the immortal wreath. Precluded now
All forms of fair and lovely on the earth
Were and dissolving from his care, like things
That in the slow fall of the northern dusk
Folded forget their edged lines and, spilt
From solid into smoke, seem sacked to view
Of substance by the predatory night;
So lapsed this world from Christ's regard. Nor yet
Within his mind found he a domicile;
For in the mind, to each the natural
Asylum from the harrowing of time,
There Jesus found but dumb and foreign forms,
Unyielding their submission to his heart,
And ruthlessness and ordeal forlorn.
Even when his dazing will longed to possess
The souls of the redeemed he scarce discerned
What thing it so desired and, in the strife
Of mind to know the object whose defect
Was torment, only knew the pang of love
Rebuked by silence and the abstinence
Of what it nameless cherished. But of all
Most grievous was that exile of the will
From quiet in the conscious sight of God,
Not merited for its decline from law
Nor for surrender of its purpose proud

Or God's (for the fulfilment of his due
Jesus might not forgo nor yet ignore),
But because even itself would pity not
The will for its own anguish, but desired
Relentless by its native liberty
To be in exile chained. So stood the will
Baffled and bound in presence of the face
Of the desired good, unskilled to seize
And in contentment to possess, but barred
Upon the threshold of the ambitioned goal,
Suppliant unavailing and in vain
Battling to apprehend. As a captive borne
To a far land to toil for alien lords
In slavery remorseless, haunted is
Noonday and night by countenances dear
And stolen long, remembered now with strength
So great of longing that the cloudy forms
Of mind betray the mind to the belief
That they are given to the eyes, until
He seeks to hold them once again and clasps
The empty air and all his misery
And shivers in the winter of despair
Unpitied, unavailing; so Christ's soul
Still by the music of the vision drawn,
Still by his will besought to follow it,
By that same will was held in interdict,
Until his being, God's to the intellect,
Assumed the guise of wraith, as impotent
To slake will's burning need as the dim shapes
Of the relinquished earth. The plenitude
Christ tasted now of utter loneliness,

Holding his will in perfect poverty
Without possession, poverty the sword
Of all his victories, now poverty
Of joy in heaven and earth and all the range
Of beauty save in his unshaken will
To abdicate its joy. And from all good
Withdrawn the mind upon itself revulsed
Its proper destitution present knew,
Drawing to itself by peremptory pain
The drifting consciousness. And as the fog
Of mortal coma tangled more the soul
It seemed to sink to death from good, from God,
The vision far becoming and more faint,
To welter yearning in a void abyss
In horrid and all-devastating flood,
The monstrous chaos of oblivion
With roar exultant for its victim voiced,
Though unsubstantial. And as the spirit seemed
To be sucked downward into emptiness
Far from fulfilment of its high desires,
It uttered through the lips its agony
Of love deferred, and the words pealed: "I thirst."
So at the last returned the bitter woe
That racked him in the garden, absolute
Privation of the goodness that his heart
Sought for its comfort. Listening at hand
A soldier, stung by sudden pity rare,
Interpreted the universal thirst
Of spirit desolate for the desire
Of the parched tongue, and on a spear upraised
A wine-drenched sop to the divine lips wide

And gasping. But, aware by the sharp taste
Of aid unwelcome in elected throes,
Averted Christ his lips though pricked by heat
Of drought imperative.

                    So in those hours
When the Judean peers and half their crew
Had gone with the indomitable wrath
That charred the glory of the Son of God
Burning upon their brows, still Jesus fought
Within, alone, unresting, that supreme
War to endure. And the dispersed groups
Of watchers on the plain slowly grew warned
Of hanging issues passing human grasp
Around them and impalpable battle waged
In dubious peril, and forgot desire
To join the city or to meditate
The common, but in silence and still poise
Continuous hung rapt on Jesus' fate
Minute by minute till two hours were sped,
While seemed the onward of the stepping sun
And numbed time to halt. And they, intent
With expectation of some manifest
Betrayal of his secret potencies
In Christ's hanged body, noted not the signs
Around of might occult in act prepared,
The ever-darkening gloom, and the gross earth
Shuddering before its blasting, but retained
In terror and inquisitive desire
Christ in their eyes and minds.

                      And in those hours
To the minds fixed immobile on one mark

Years seemed to wither, histories to pass
And the brisk world wax senile, as its tale
Its climax neared and in top course itself
Revisited the glory of its birth,
Won from captivity by the death divine
And the will firm in anguish. And at last
The time was born determined by Christ's will
The term of all his throes, and now brought forth
To being by his steadfastness, on which
Hung all the health and hope of the ruined world
And method to rebirth; and as it touched
The last ascension of his agony,
When flesh was spent and the beleaguering hours
Weary and laggard at the constancy
Unwearied of the unbreakable resolve
To dare their malices, then from his lips
A thunderous deathcry of late victory
And sternly carried, "It is finished," burst.
This was the point to which all years had bent
Desirous, since the perfidy of Eve
Gave forfeit of her children's high entail,
The woe of Eden and the desert borne
Upon the garden and the happy bowers.
Finished were all the promises of God
From age to age renewed, with stricter aim
Ever on the heroic evidence
And the disaster laureled of the cross
Pointed, to feed the languor of assent
In man and faltering purpose, by the strong
Motive of God's relief foretold; therewith
Finished the task wrought by the strength of God,

Insuperable else, to bear unmoved
Pain ruining in every faculty,
The body's bruising slow, and manifold
Man's means to wring the soul, which in the heat
Of ordeal must by the sight of God
Remain uncomforted. Now at the word
Of Christ's will, lessor of his passive sense
To his tormentors, master therewithal
Absolute of his captors and their gains,
His passion, as of the universal grief
And greed of creatures, was foreclosed the reign
Of cruelty on his manhood; and instead
Invisible presences in session thronged
About his head, exulting in his crown.
There Victory stood, and Grace with winged gifts,
And Freedom grasping her live fetters rent,
The serpent, Patience with her golden clock,
And sworded Chivalry, and many more
Of metaphysical servants that endow
The heirs of the heroic cross with strength
Invincible, and the Church evertried
Make everlasting. And the angelic host
Arose from hooded vigil and repose
Tense with strange care, and, by the cross erect
In triumph and stern joy, made to salute
Him who by suffering had achieved the deed
Most valorous and most beneficent
Of all the deeds of men. But in the soul
Of Christ the sceptered will that summoned death
Dropped at its call the bonds that barred its flight
Bent for the bliss superb, and poised it girt

To leap from life to everlasting life
And crown earth's king anew. And with the free
Speech of a princely vassal that disdains
Homage but to the Highest, willingly,
For love not fear, but rather as one gives
Proudly that in his suzerain has part
And right, He gave tithe of his life: "Father,
Into your hands I recommend my soul."
Slow dropped the words, then straight the bruised head
Dropped trembling, and the body from the nails
Sagged and was quiet, of the soul forlorn,
And Christ was dead and man was born again.

Then indignation seized the face of things,
And frowned the heavens more when the red orb
Of thwarted day into a cell of gloom
Rolled from the steep sky sheer and its haught seat
Inert, and, in untimely course reduced,
Night's raven plume swept from the gaunt hills down
Upon the city, guarding its savage brood.
And staggered all the buxom breast of earth
As it were quick with mortal throes and roared
Through all the caverns of the underworld,
And cracked and vomited great smoking rocks
From its profound into the tottering works
Of man and nature. Near the peak of doom
A sepulcher stood dazzling in the murk,
And suddenly tossed by the quaking world
Sundered and cast its door; and through the breach
A form in tatters of rent cerements strode
And stood with blind and moveless face of rage

Uttering mute accusation. And the last crowds,
Now terrified, shrieked and with covered eyes
Fled headlong from the plain, most to the gates,
But some into the wilderness of fields,
Falling amongst the boulders and the trees
But still unstayed in effort. Stood alone
Rome's iron soldiery, though pale and grim
And silent all, save the centurion;
He, having seen, now with defeated heart
Muttered, while all Christ's mourners heeded him.
"Truly this was the Son of God, a man
Of blameless deeds."
                         Meanwhile against the flux
Of fugitives there from the city came
A band of three, one a decurion
And the prince, Nicodemus, and the lord
Of Arimathea, Joseph. On the rock
To the centurion the soldier spoke:
"The Procurator sends me with the charge
To haste these culprits' deaths and from the roods
Removed to hide the dead. This afternoon
One cried in the Antonia 'Christ is dead,'
And forthwith unto Pilate came these lords
Foretelling riot for the dead untombed
Upon the Sabbath and demanded straight
Surrender of Christ's body to bestow
In Joseph's newcut vault. Pilate deferred,
Though hardly, to their high authority,
And bade me go with them and break the bones
Of the two living; 'Nor spare Christ,' he said
(For he is now all savage and his old

Forbearance quite forgone), 'if he be dead
Indeed yet pierce his heart that all may know
This world is free of him.' Now must I these
Perform, then render to these lords the due
Of their concession." Then the centurion
Bowed silent but with formidable eyes
Of quelled revolt, and his companion drew
His cudgel and addressed him to the thieves
And with one stroke smashed the long shins of one
Who yelled out once and died, but Dismas died
Under the blow nor wakened from his trance.
But Christ was dead so the decurion
Lunged strongly with his spear beneath the ribs
Into the quiet heart; and from the rent
Much blood and water poured. But he within
Felt sudden sorrow from the fairness marred
And Christ betrayed by his exceeding love.

Then tedded Nicodemus on the rock
His freight of windingbands, aloes, and myrrh,
Sweet spices for the burial, and raised
An iron claw to grip the buried nails
And strongly drew one forth. And the hand fell
Dead, and the body drooped, and the fair head
Sank forward on the steelclad shoulderblade
Of the centurion, with the blood divine
Arrosing its white sheen. Then one more hand
And last the feet were freed, and in the arms
Of John and the won soldier Christ was borne
To earth. There was a chamber hewn below
A hundred paces from the pedestal

Of crucifixion, where some cypresses
Subdued the hectic dusk to night's abyss;
Thither did John and the Judean lords
Bear Jesus, while his mother and the two
Women with trappings for the burial
Mourning came after.

                But at the sepulcher
Sat Mary and received him in her lap,
And on one hand propped the grave, dangling head
And put with one the tresses from his brow,
And looked on him as to reproach his sleep
Long, long, then weeping said: "Untimely tears,
For mourning is unkind when it regrets
An end so generous to a life so pure;
Death though it seals achievement here completes
And leaves it indefectible in us
To stir immortal gladness. But what joy
Even in that fufilment can abide
This witness of irrevocable farewell
That in my arms you leave, beloved child?
Now while I gaze upon these beaten limbs
And credit your extinction and discern
The desolation of this empty world,
All thought is banished but the memory
Of you who were my all. Was this my son?
Are these the lips, pupils long since of mine,
That marveling I once beheld astir
With the new spirit and declaring heard
Of childish wants and trust insoluble
In my weak motherhood, now wrung and loose
And of their young breath cold? Are these the limbs

That once to my embrace sprang quick and fond,
Now hanging from it as by bitter toil
Outwearied and into perpetual sleep
Cast irredeemably? Is this the blood
That once at noble tales kindled this cheek
But hides its pallor now? O these remains
Like trophies of the fall make palpable
The devastated prime and vanished joy
More than the wintry emptiness of loss
That leaves no monument. The lance that bores
Your heart now pierces mine and wounds the world
That now has slain its glory. Come the dark,
Come cold, silence and death! Without your eyes
All things to me already are in cold,
Death, silence and the dark. And to your tomb
My mind now journeys with its slain desire,
My only son, extinguished but for thought
Counting the watches of your change until
God shall revoke your life. Forgive me, dear,
If I forget your Godhead, who must mourn
Human my only child. The creature bows
To the just will, and with thanksgiving takes
The pledge of a new union that shall last
Beyond all time after this parting brief;
But all the woman grieves for gladness dead
Which known must seem to dreams of fantasy
More worth than the unknown. You were to me
So dear that other happiness with you
Or any sorrow was impossible
And equal were all fortunes; night and day
Were bright with you and spring filled all the year;

To be with you made imperceptible
All other company and poverty
One with exceeding wealth. To your dear youth
These tears, this gaze of eyes, and this last kiss
On these poor shards of you now bid farewell
Forever. Let us shorten mourning now
Since the whole heaven is in festival
This day at the high prowess of his cross
And let us to our offices to bind
His limbs with homage for his lonely rest,
For he was royal and dies but for a space."

So spoke the virgin mother and long gazed
As if by will to make the dead eyes quick,
Then laid him down upon the linen bands.
But they fetched water from the garden well
And bathed his gaping wounds and clotted hair
And with their spices laid to breast and limbs
Wound deftly in one fragrant cloth the whole
From feet to head. Then to the hollow rock
They bore him with their stricken eyes of cloud
Held prisoners to his face; there they laid down
His limbs on the stone table and composed
His body as for sleep and, with set eyes
Averted lest the longing for his face
Should hold their going, passed without. The men
There doffed their cloaks and to the portal stone
Set brawny arms and shoulders tense until
It groaned and scarcely stirred to their grave stress
Then tottered to its socket in the mouth
And rocked to gradual rest. They with toil swinked

Sighed and put on their cloaks and took the thorns
And nails, and for a while lingered at gaze
Upon the hallowed tomb sealed and the rock,
Naked and desert, topped with crosses three
That loomed more dark against the rising dark,
Filling the sullen void with memory
And vast and shadowy surmise. Then all
Went silent and forlorn with halting steps
And minds astonished to the city gates.

THE END